LEADERS

LEADERS
STRATEGIES FOR
TAKING CHARGE

SECOND EDITION

Warren Bennis & Burt Nanus

HarperBusiness
A Division of HarperCollinsPublishers

First HarperBusiness paperback edition published 1997.

Library of Congress Cataloging-in-Publication Data
Bennis, Warren G.
    Leaders : strategies for taking charge / by Warren
 Bennis and Burt Nanus. — 2nd ed.
      p. cm.
    Includes bibliographical references and index.
    ISBN 0-88730-839-2
    1. Leadership. 2. Executive ability. I. Nanus, Burt.
II. Title.
HD57.7B46   1997
658.4'092—DC21   96-47290

02 03 04 05   ◆/RRD 20 19 18 17 16 15

To our children:
Kate
John
and
Will
and
Leora
and all children:
leaders of the next generation

CONTENTS

FOREWORD TO THE SECOND EDITION

We look back with pride on the first edition of *Leaders* with all the "objectivity" authors can summon up on their past work and think that many of our concepts—on vision, empowerment, organizational learning and trust, for example—are as valid today as they were twelve years ago. On the other hand, upon rereading the first edition, we found a number of things we feel we should have emphasized more strongly. The French have a phrase for this: *l'esprit d'escalier*, literally, the spirit of the staircase—the things we wish we had said as we walk down the steps after a meeting. So we decided to update the earlier version of the book, adding new material here and there and a whole new section in the last chapter on our ideas about the future of leadership. Here's what we want to emphasize.

1: *Leadership is about character.* Character is a continuously evolving thing. The process of becoming a leader is much the same as becoming an integrated human being.

When you look at the typical criteria that most organizations use to evaluate their executives, there are usually seven: technical competence, people skills, conceptual skills, track record, taste, judgment and character. Of these, the last two are the most difficult to identify, measure or develop. We certainly don't know how to teach them: Business schools barely try. We do know how they're formed. What's interesting is that although a lot of executives are derailed (or plateaued) for lack of character or judgment, we've never observed a premature career-ending for lack of technical competence. Ironically, what's most important in leadership can't be easily quantified.

2: *To keep organizations competitive, leaders must be instrumental in creating a social architecture capable of generating intellectual capital.* What matters most about the structure, architecture or design of the organization is that it exemplify Rosabeth Moss Kanter's 4 F's: focused, flexible, fast and friendly. We'd like to add a fifth F: fun. Almost any architecture will work if the people want it to work. We're less concerned about structure than about what leaders do to motivate and create a culture of respect, caring and trust.

Organizations—today especially—are about ideas, innovation, imagination, creativity—intellectual capital. The brightest leaders are aware of this. Percy Barnevik, chairman of the giant ABB, tells us that "releasing the brain power" is his biggest challenge. Disney's Michael Eisner, especially when referring to his feature animation group, says that "my inventory goes home at night."

3: *We cannot exaggerate the significance of a strong determination to achieve a goal or realize a vision—a conviction, even a passion.* Max DePree, former chairman of the Herman Miller company, once said that "the first task of a leader is to define reality." That's another way of talking about purpose and direction. Without a sense of alignment behind that common purpose, the company is in trouble. The opposite of purpose is aimlessness, drifting. But it can't be any old purpose that will animate, galvanize and energize the people. It has to have resonance, meaning.

Our favorite example of meaning comes from a "Peanuts" cartoon strip. Lucy asks Schroeder—Schroeder playing the piano, of course, and ignoring Lucy—if he knows what love is. Schroeder stands at attention and intones, "Love: a noun, referring to a deep, intense, ineffable feeling toward another person or persons." He then sits down and returns to his piano. The last caption shows Lucy looking off in the distance, balefully saying, "On paper, he's great." Most mission statements suffer that same fate: On paper, they're great.

So the purpose has to have meaning and relevance to the followers—or else it's meaningless. In *Henry*

IV, Part I, Shakespeare has the Welsh seer, Glendower, boast to Hotspur, "I can call spirits from the vasty deep." Hotspur deflates him with "Why, so can I or so can any man; But will they come when you call for them?"

4: *The capacity to generate and sustain trust is the central ingredient in leadership.* You can have the most glorious vision in the world and it won't mean a thing if there's low trust in the organization. The trust factor is the social glue that keeps any system together. It's hard to gain and easy to lose.

We received a letter from a Fortune 500 CEO not long ago who wrote, "We've got thousands of folks, union workers and others, who want the world to be the way it used to be, and they are very unwilling to accept any alternative forecast of the future." The real problem with this company is that there is no trust in the CEO and top leadership of the firm. The CEO is an old-fashioned command-and-control type who is unable to generate trust among the key stakeholders. The union isn't the problem. He is. Ironically, this leader is one of the most venturesome in his industry, but without trust, he can't call the spirits from the vasty deep.

Tom Friedman, in the November 12, 1995, issue of the *New York Times,* writing about Yitzhak Rabin's assassination, noted the secret of Rabin's success: "Mr. Rabin had the most important attribute of leadership—authenticity. He put on no airs, he wore no masks, what you saw was what you got." The Israeli people knew they could believe Rabin and they trusted him implicitly to do the right thing. Without that trust, it would have been impossible for Rabin to make the highly risky concessions that were needed to move the peace process with the PLO forward.

5: *True leaders have an uncanny way of enrolling people in their vision through their optimism— sometimes unwarranted optimism.* For them, the glass is not half-full, it's brimming. They believe—all of the exemplary leaders we have studied—that they can change the world or, at the very least, make a dent in the universe.

They're all purveyors of hope. Confucius said that leaders are "dealers in hope." Former President Ronald Reagan embodied this outlook—call it positive illusions if you like—as well as anybody since the days of FDR, even after he was shot in an attempted assassination. Richard Wirthlin, Reagan's pollster for six years, tells the story of how, in 1982, at the depths of the depression, he came into the Oval Office with his semimonthly report. He told Reagan the bad news: "Thirty-two percent approval rating—the worst ever for any sitting president in the second year in office." Reagan reportedly smiled and said, "Dick, Dick . . . stop worrying. I'll just go out and try to get shot again."

6: *Leaders have a bias toward action that results in success.* It is the capacity to translate vision and purpose into reality. It's not enough just to have vision, trust and optimism. The leader has to manifest concrete, active steps—execution—to bring about results. Leaders make things happen. They know how to "close." As Steve Jobs once said during the heyday of the Mac computer, "real leaders ship." There must be continuous focus on the task till the work is done.

All of this reminds us that our own work on leadership isn't yet done. We had more thoughts as we went down the staircase. Our favorite philosopher, "the great one," Wayne Gretzky, put it best when he said, "You miss one hundred percent of the shots you don't take." That's why we're taking another shot in this book.

Warren Bennis and Burt Nanus
Santa Monica, California
August 1996

ACKNOWLEDGMENTS

Ralph Waldo Emerson used to greet old friends whom he hadn't seen in a while with the following salutation: "What's become clear to you since we last met?" An acknowledgment section provides authors the opportunity to reflect on that question and to bestow overdue appreciation to those who, during the course of writing and rewriting, may have been forgotten or lost sight of, but who now—it becomes clear to us—must be identified and thanked. Because our book has been a truly collaborative effort, we make this acknowledgment in the same spirit, a duet of praise.

First and foremost, we must single out the ninety leaders who participated in this study without whom this book would not have been undertaken, written or finished. They have been generous company. We also have to point to John Gardner, Donald Michael and James MacGregor Burns for their intellectual inspiration. Plagiarism and emulation have a lot in common, though the former is both a cardinal sin and a legal insult and the latter is, as they say, the highest form of flattery for which we hope to be forgiven.

A lot of people have been our intellectual goads, helping us with ideas and prodding us with their pneumatic impatience with questions like: "What about the book? What about the book?" They damned near became something of a public nuisance, but God knows when this book would have been completed if it weren't for their generous impatience as well as for their infuriating spurs. Without question the chief offenders in this respect have been Jim O'Toole, Rosabeth Moss Kanter, Werner Erhard, Tom Peters, Selwyn Enzer, Eppie Lederer, Bob Townsend and Bob Schwartz.

A special note of thanks must go to both Mary Jane O'Donnell and Marcia Wilkof for their conceptual contributions to our book: Mary Jane for introducing us to the meaning of the Amazing Wallendas and Marcia Wilkof for her seminal contribution to the chapter on Strategy II.

Doris MacPherson not only typed and retyped numberless copies of the book but provided unsolicited (but always sound) suggestions about how to improve our efforts. Debbie Rangel and Sheila Thomas also good-naturedly tested the limits of word processing with frequent drafts and Freda Maltin handled administrative details with grace.

There are four others we feel obliged to thank for their incredible patience with us and their solid support during the two and a half years this book has been in the making: Dean Jack Steele, our "boss" at USC, who has been unswerving in his support;

Marlene Nanus, for her quiet devotion to a husband "in labor"; Bill Leigh for reasons that he will privately understand; and to our editor, Harriet Rubin, with whom we arm-wrestled and fought and worked until she finally won her argument, making this the best possible book we were capable of making it.

Warren Bennis
Burt Nanus

MISTAKING CHARGE

These are the hard times in
which a genius would wish to live.
Great necessities call forth great leaders.

Abigail Adams
1790, in a letter to
Thomas Jefferson

"Leadership" is a word on everyone's lips. The young attack it and the old grow wistful for it. Parents have lost it and police seek it. Experts claim it and artists spurn it, while scholars want it. Philosophers reconcile it (as authority) with liberty and theologians demonstrate its compatibility with conscience. If bureaucrats pretend they have it, politicians wish they did. Everybody agrees that there is less of it than there used to be. The matter now stands as a certain

Mr. Wildman thought it stood in 1648: "Leadership hath been broken into pieces."

At the same time, history effervesces with the names of individuals who have provided extraordinary leadership and risen to the challenges of their eras: Winston Churchill. Mahatma Gandhi. Golda Meir. Franklin D. Roosevelt. Their leadership built great nations. Tom Watson. Edwin Land. Alfred P. Sloan. Their leadership built great organizations.

Often the enormousness of present-day challenges and the pace of change seem unaccompanied by great notions and the great people to implement them. This void, like so many darknesses, may augur new leaders. And certainly in this moratorium new concepts of leadership have incubated. With the emergence of great men and women we can anticipate exciting new visions of power.

The need was never so great. A chronic crisis of governance—that is, the pervasive incapacity of organizations to cope with the expectations of their constituents—is now an overwhelming factor worldwide. If there was ever a moment in history when a comprehensive strategic view of leadership was needed, not just by a few leaders in high office but by large numbers of leaders in every job, from the factory floor to the executive suite, from a McDonald's fast-food franchise to a law firm, this is certainly it.

This book was written in the belief that leadership is the pivotal force behind successful organizations and that to create vital and viable organizations, leadership is necessary to help organizations develop a new vision of what they can be, then mobilize the organization to change toward the new vision. General Motors, AT&T, Citicorp, IBM, Chase Manhattan, Disney, Eastman Kodak and G.E. represent a partial sample of major U.S. corporations investing in major organizational transformations to ensure long-term vitality. The main stem-winder, in all cases, is the leadership. The new leader, which is what this book is about, is one who commits people to action, who converts followers into leaders, and who may convert leaders into agents of change. We refer to this as "transformative leadership" and will return to this concept throughout.[1]

But before going any further, we'd like to say a few things about leadership and today's managerial context, which makes leadership so problematic.

A NEW THEORY OF LEADERSHIP

Through the years, our view of what leadership is and who can exercise it has changed considerably. Leadership competencies have remained constant, but our understanding of what it is, how it works, and the ways in which people learn to apply it has shifted. We do have the beginnings of a general theory of leadership, from history and social research and above all from the ruminations of reflective practitioners such as Moses, Pericles, Julius Caesar, Jesus Christ, Martin Luther, Niccolò Machiavelli and James Madison, and in our own time from such disparate sources of wisdom as Gandhi, V. I. Lenin, Harriet Tubman, Winston Churchill, Eleanor Roosevelt, Charles de Gaulle, Dean

Acheson, Mao Tse-tung, Chester Barnard, Martin Luther King, Jr., John Gardner and Henry Kissinger, who have very little in common except that they have not only been there but tried with some candor to speculate on paper about it.

But folklore and reflective observation are not enough except to convince us that leaders are physically strong and abnormally hard workers. Today we are a little closer to understanding how and who people lead, but it wasn't easy getting there. Decades of academic analysis have given us more than 850 definitions of leadership. Literally thousands of empirical investigations of leaders have been conducted in the last seventy-five years alone, but no clear and unequivocal understanding exists as to what distinguishes leaders from nonleaders, and perhaps more important, what distinguishes *effective* leaders from *ineffective* leaders and *effective* organizations from *ineffective* organizations.

Never have so many labored so long to say so little. Multiple interpretations of leadership exist, each providing a sliver of insight but each remaining an incomplete and wholly inadequate explanation. Most of these definitions don't agree with each other, and many of them would seem quite remote to the leaders whose skills are being dissected. Definitions reflect fads, fashions, political tides and academic trends. They don't always reflect reality and sometimes they just represent nonsense. It's as if what Braque once said about art is also true of leadership: "The only thing that matters in art is the part that cannot be explained."

Leadership skills were once thought a matter of birth. Leaders were born, not made, summoned to their calling through some unfathomable process. This might be called the "Great Man" theory of leadership. It saw power as being vested in a very limited number of people whose inheritance and destiny made them leaders. Those of the right breed could lead; all others must be led. Either you had it or you didn't. No amount of learning or yearning could change your fate.

When this view failed to explain leadership, it was replaced by the notion that great events made leaders of otherwise ordinary people. Presumably Lenin was just "milling about" when a revolution pounced on his deliberations, and Washington was simply "on hand" when the colonies opted for countrydom. This "Big Bang" idea in which the situation and the followers combined to make a leader, like the "Great Man" theory, was another inadequate definition.

Like love, leadership continued to be something everyone knew existed but nobody could define. Many other theories of leadership have come and gone. Some looked at the leader. Some looked at the situation. None has stood the test of time. With such a track record, it is understandable why leadership research and theory have been so frustrating as to deserve the label "the La Brea Tar Pits" of organizational inquiry. Located in Los Angeles, these asphalt pits house the remains of a long sequence of prehistoric animals that came to investigate but never left the area.

Now, in a stasis uninterrupted by either Great Men or Big Bangs, we have a new opportunity to appraise our leaders and ponder the essence of power.

These days power is conspicuous in its absence. Powerlessness in the face of crisis. Powerlessness in the face of complexity. With contradiction and polarization of thought and action, power has been sabotaged while a kind of plodding pandemonium surges. Institutions have been rigid, slothful or mercurial. Supposed leaders seem ignorant and out of touch, insensitive and unresponsive. Worst of all, solutions have been jerrybuilt or they have not been built at all.

THE CONTEXT OF LEADERSHIP

All of which has created a managerial mayhem that can be more fully understood only if we examine the leadership environment of today. That can be summarized under three major contexts: *commitment, complexity* and *credibility*.

Commitment

Public Agenda Forum[2] undertook a major survey of the American nonmanagerial workforce in the early '80s with the following disturbing results:

- Fewer than 1 out of every 4 jobholders said that they were working at full potential.
- One half said they did not put effort into their job over and above what was required to hold on to it.

- The overwhelming majority, 75 percent, said that they could be significantly more effective than they presently were.
- Close to 6 out of 10 Americans on the job believed that they "do not work as hard as they used to."

In the absence of strong commitment, these workers proved unable to compete successfully with their hardworking and lower paid counterparts in Japan and Southeast Asia. Rather than inspire and energize them, however, America's business leaders chose simply to fire workers by the tens of thousands in wave after wave of "downsizing." As a result, in place of companies with underutilized workers, we now have a society in which millions of laid-off people are working below their capacity, many in part-time or dead-end jobs.

As many as half the surviving workers now report the opposite problem—heavy workloads, long hours, and high stress. But while fear of job loss may make some employees work harder today, loyalty to employers and job commitment seem to have decreased even further. Workers feel powerless. Few of them are willing to become fully engaged in a work situation and go the extra mile for an employer who regards them as easily expendable.

People talk about the decline of the work ethic. They complain that enough scientists and engineers are not being trained. But what really exists is a *commitment gap*. Leaders have failed to instill vision, meaning and trust in their followers. They have failed to empower them. Regardless of whether we're looking at organizations, government agencies, institutions or small enterprises, the key and pivotal factor needed to enhance human resources is leadership.

Complexity

This is an era marked by rapid and spastic change. The problems of organizations are increasingly complex. There are too many ironies, polarities, dichotomies, dualities, ambivalences, paradoxes, confusions, contradictions, contraries and messes for any organization to understand and deal with. One can pick up a paper any day of the week and find indications of this inordinate complexity. To illustrate, we noted the following stories in the *Wall Street Journal* during one five-day period in mid-1996.

- G. E. Capital bought First Colony, a life insurance firm, for $11 billion; seven other acquisitions of more than a billion dollars each were announced, as well as many smaller ones.
- In a stunning discovery, space scientists found strong evidence of ancient life on Mars, boosting chances of a great new expansion in space exploration.
- China faced a banking crisis, with at least a third of all its loans nonperforming. The World Bank called China's banking system "technically bankrupt."
- The recruiting frenzy for high-technology

workers intensified, touching off hiring wars that resembled the scramble for basketball stars. Meantime, as many as 40 percent of public sector workers in some cities lost their well-paying jobs because of outsourcing to the private sector where the same jobs pay much less.

- European drug companies accounted for 58 percent of all major new investment in U.S. biotechnology firms in the past eighteen months.
- The Energy Department awarded $11 billion in contracts to clean up nuclear waste sites in Washington and South Carolina. Meanwhile, the E.P.A. issued standards covering emissions from outboard motors.
- America On-Line said it had more than six million subscribers, up sixfold in just two years. Meanwhile, Microsoft and Verifone became partners on software for retailing over the Internet, and 3M launched Imation, a new $2.25 billion firm in the information and imaging field.
- The U.S. House of Representatives passed a strong antiterrorism bill.
- Malaysia, in a bid to attract high-technology firms, set up a 300-square-mile area with an advanced information technology infrastructure and enticing tax and other incentives.
- The Daewoo Group of South Korea entered the U.S. car market, planning to sell at least 100,000 vehicles by the year 2000.

Newspapers indicate similarly portentous events daily. These changes have profound effects on our society and on how we lead our organizations. They are interactive, discontinuous and accelerating. Traditional information sources and management techniques have become less effective or obsolete. Linear information, linear thinking and incremental strategies are no match for the turbulence of today's business climate. Extrapolating fails to recognize new unknowns. And "temporizing" solves nothing.

A metaphor for the times we're living in, particularly the managerial environment, is "Chinese baseball," as related to us by R. Tsiu. Chinese baseball is played exactly like American baseball with one major exception, and that is this: The minute the ball leaves the pitcher's hand, the fielders can do anything they want. They can actually mass the bases and put them all together. They can separate second and third base by another thirty yards if they like. All the fielders for a weak hitter can edge toward the infield; for a power hitter the entire team can play close to the fences; for a slower runner, first base can be extended to the outfield. It's crazy—seemingly. And that's the way things appear right now, with little reason to expect simpler times in the future. Leave those hopes to cowboy movies and nostalgia buffs. Alfred North Whitehead cautioned us wisely in this respect when he said: "Seek simplicity and then distrust it." The trouble is that too many seek simplicity and then forget to distrust it. "I predict a bright future for complexity," said a character in an E. B. White short story written almost seventy-five years ago. And the character went on to complete his sentence and summarize our present condition:

"Have you ever considered how complicated things can get, what with one thing always leading to another?"

In some quarters the complexity has led to what appears to be a collective intolerance of ambiguity and a "credibility gap," which we now turn to.

Credibility

Credibility is at a premium these days. Leaders are being scrutinized as never before. Fifty years ago this was not the case. The public sector has grown more voracious and vociferous since World War II. Attention to welfare, social services, health, education and the environment has spawned a morass of advocacy groups, government regulations, organized consumers and unions to whom the media is ever more responsive. All are questioning and challenging authority, and powerful people must move with the caution of alley cats negotiating minefields.

External forces as well as teeming inner constituencies impinge and impose on all organizations and their leaders. Current public sector "checkpoints" leave little leeway for anything but rectitude and responsibility. Valid, important and constructive ideas have fallen prey to disclosure and criticism. Public relations has become bigger business than Business itself while leaders attempt to summon and sway refractory and capricious opinions.

The information age has hatched a public awareness rendering the managerial environment a kind of media-controlled petri dish. Although mass com-

munications is very possibly the blight of managerial impulse, it is also inevitable. When a man or a
woman opts for leadership and assumes responsibility, he or she also surrenders privacy. Just as a mole-
cule of great mass acquires more atoms, leaders will
attract more stakeholders and more observation. The
vexing paradox here is "How do you get everybody
into the act and still get some action?" (We'll have
more to say about this form of complexity later on.)

Deep feelings of insecurity are the norm. They are
experienced by people from all belief systems and economic brackets, all spheres of influence and all levels
of competency. Several years ago we saw bumper stickers saying simply "Impeach Someone." This seemed to
epitomize the situation. During the last election
bumper stickers read "Don't Vote. It Will Only
Encourage Them." This attitude, shared by so many
nervous Americans, is as much indicative of a reluc-
tant followership as a scarcity of leaders. In short, it is
the leader/follower transaction that has gone awry.

PARADIGM SHIFTS

The contexts of apathy, escalating change and uncertainty make leadership seem like maneuvering over
ever faster and more undirected ball bearings.
Dispiritedness has risen as we have traversed the
wicked slalom of the last twenty years. But in spite
of the mediocrities, travesties, trespasses, destruc-
tions and dislocations of the last two decades, we
believe, with many contemporary thinkers, that it is

not with stupor that the American people suffer anxiety and even nonallegiance. Rather, it is that we are approaching a major turning point in history—what Karl Jaspers referred to as an "axial point," where some new height of vision is sought, where some fundamental redefinitions are required, where our table of values will have to be reviewed. We seek lives not measured solely in terms of income, societies not assessed on gasoline consumption, and freedom from that most beguiling and misleading of all valuations, the GNP.

The fact is that as difficult, frustrating and fearful as these times are, they are also interesting, catalytic and crucial. "It is," as the fox said to the Little Prince, "not what it appears to be." A new paradigm is being born.

Survival in this seeming madness calls for great flexibility and awareness on the part of leaders and followers alike. Our larger objectives, peace and prosperity, must pivot on increased communication and broadened belief systems. We must fix our horizons not on the mandates of atrophying institutions but on the successes of burgeoning new enterprises. It is to the trends we should all look as we shape the future and as we shape ourselves.

Chronicler John Naisbitt isolated ten present and future persuasions in *Megatrends*, his bestselling description of the new paradigm.[3] The changes are as follows:

From	To
Industrial Society	Information Society
Forced Technology	High Tech/High Touch
National Economy	World Economy

Short Term	Long Term
Centralization	Decentralization
Institutional Help	Self-Help
Representative Democracy	Participatory Democracy
Hierarchies	Networking
North	South
Either/Or	Multiple Option

These changes have been examined, in one form or another, for some time. This includes "oldies" such as McGregor's "Theory Y,"[4] Townsend's *Up the Organization*,[5] Slater's "New Culture,"[6] and Salk's "Epoch B."[7] More recently, this paradigm shift can be observed in Prigogine's *Dissipative Structures*,[8] Peters's *Thriving on Chaos*,[9] Drucker's *The New Realities*[10] and Handy's *The Age of Paradox*.[11]

However, there is something missing—one issue that has been systematically neglected without exception: *POWER, the basic energy to initiate and sustain action translating intention into reality,* the quality without which leaders cannot lead. Just as the economists have painted themselves into a narrowing corner by failing to recognize the limitations and constraints of the free market, so too have students of organizations avoided the nucleus of leadership. Without any qualification, we can bluntly state that most of the current paradigms of organizational life, be they the "new age" variety or the older brands, have failed to consider *power*.*

---

*An important and seminal exception is Rosabeth Moss Kanter's book, *The Change Masters*, which deals directly and masterfully with power.[12]

Bertrand Russell once said, "The fundamental concept in social science is power, in the same sense in which energy is the fundamental concept in physics." Our ignorance of this, our forest-for-the-trees blindness, has led to human transactional short-circuitry. In short, we are a nation suffering from a serious power blockage.

Ironically, power is one of the most familiar forces in the universe. It is the pull and push we all experience and exercise from birth to death. It is implicit in all human interaction—familial, sexual, occupational, national and international—either covertly or overtly.

However, this basic social energy has been embroidered upon beyond recognition. It carries with it a host of connotations incurred over thousands of years. These implications—including avarice, insensitivity, cruelty, corruption—have led in aggregate to the disregard and disintegration of power across the board. In other words, power is at once the most necessary and most distrusted element exigent to human progress.

To understand this ambiguity, observe the ways in which power has been misused. Historically leaders have controlled rather than organized, administered repression rather than expression, and held their followers in arrestment rather than in evolution.

We *are* going forward, but we are doing so without affording power a place in our new vision. Our fear of confrontation—whether between lovers or friends or through crime, local injustices, the media or government—has slowed and in some cases stymied participation in a just future. Like homeowners who hesitate to call the exterminator because they're afraid when the termites stop holding hands the house will fall down, *the paradox of any progress based on conflict is its ultimate fragility.*

We must learn to perceive power for what it really is. Basically, it's the reciprocal of leadership. Perhaps the best way to illustrate how we understand it is to use an illustration, and the best one that comes to mind is that of Lee Iacocca at Chrysler. He provided the leadership to transform a company from bankruptcy to success. He created a vision of success and mobilized large factions of key employees to align behind that vision. Almost exclusively because of Iacocca's leadership, by 1983 Chrysler made a profit, boosted employee morale, and helped employees generate a sense of meaning in their work. He empowered them. The effects weren't transitory, either—by 1995, Chrysler was the world's lowest-cost auto maker, with annual earnings of $2 billion and the highest profit margin of America's Big Three auto makers.

In fact, we believe that Iacocca's high visibility symbolizes the missing element in management today (and much of management theory) in that his style of leadership is central to organizational success. Our concept of power and leadership, then, is modeled on the Iacocca phenomenon: Power is the basic energy needed to initiate and sustain action or, to put it another way, the *capacity to translate intention into reality and sustain it.* Leadership is the wise use of this power: *Transformative* leadership.*

As we view it, effective leadership can move organizations from current to future states, create visions of potential opportunities for organizations, instill within employees commitment to change and instill new cultures and strategies in organizations that mobilize and focus energy and resources. These leaders are not born. They emerge when organizations face new problems and complexities that cannot be solved by unguided evolution. They assume responsibilities for reshaping organizational practices to adapt to environmental changes. They direct organizational changes that build confidence and empower their employees to seek new ways of doing things. They overcome resistance to change by creating visions of the future that evoke confidence in and mastery of new organizational practices. Over the next decade or two, the leadership we are talking about and will refer to throughout this book will become more evident in organizations able to respond to spastic and turbulent conditions.

We do face an uncertain and unsettling future, but not one without vision. Vision is the commodity of leaders, and power is their currency. We are at a critical point in our nation's history and we cannot go back as individuals or as a country to what we were ten, five or even one year ago. The future is now and it's our turn.

*We are indebted here and throughout this book to the seminal work of James MacGregor Burns and especially want to note his contributions to our work.[13]

LEADING OTHERS, MANAGING YOURSELF

Among the most difficult questions about any radical paradigmatic shift are these: What do you do in the meantime? How do you prepare? What is the role of leaders and educators? These questions are simultaneously problematic and marvelous.

In an effort to better understand and participate in this age of change, we undertook the subject of leadership as the central ingredient to the way progress is created and to the way organizations develop and survive. A series of ninety interviews were conducted, sixty with successful CEOs, all corporate presidents or chairmen of boards, and thirty with outstanding leaders from the public sector.

Since leadership is the most studied and least understood topic of any in the social sciences, a context for the interviews had to be created. Books on leadership are often as majestically useless as they are pretentious. Leadership is like the Abominable Snowman, whose footprints are everywhere but who is nowhere to be seen. Not wanting to further muddle the bewildering melange of leadership definitions, we set out to provide a unique and instructive framework for our investigation: the present.

It almost seems trite to say it, but we must state the obvious. Present problems will not be solved without successful organizations, and organizations cannot be successful without effective leadership. Now.

A business short on capital can borrow money, and one with a poor location can move. But a business short on leadership has little chance for survival. It will be reduced to the controls of, at best, efficient clerks in narrow orbits. Organizations must be led to overcome their "trained incapacity" and to adapt to changing conditions. Leadership is what gives an organization its vision and its ability to translate that vision into reality. Without this translation, a transaction between leaders and followers, there is no organizational heartbeat.

The study pursued leaders who have achieved fortunate mastery over present confusion—in contrast to those who simply react, throw up their hands, and live in a perpetual state of "present shock."

The problem with many organizations, and especially the ones that are failing, is that they tend to be overmanaged and underled (see figure 1). They may excel in the ability to handle the daily routine, yet never question whether the routine should be done at all. There is a profound difference between management and leadership, and both are important. "To manage" means "to bring about, to accomplish, to have charge of or responsibility for, to conduct." "Leading" is "influencing, guiding in direction, course, action, opinion." The distinction is crucial. *Managers are people who do things right and leaders are people who do the right thing.* The difference may be summarized as activities of vision and judgment—*effectiveness*—versus activities of mastering routines—*efficiency*.

note!

Thus, the context of leadership that all those interviewed both shared and embodied was directly related to how they *construed* their roles. They viewed themselves as leaders, not managers. This is to say that they concerned themselves with their organizations' basic purposes and general direction. Their perspective was "vision-oriented." They did not spend their time on the "how tos," the proverbial "nuts and bolts," but rather with the paradigms of action, with "doing the right thing."

Furthermore, the study concentrated on leaders directing the new trends. There were no "incrementalists." These were people creating new ideas, new policies, new methodologies. They changed the basic metabolism of their organizations. These leaders were, in Camus's phrase, "creating dangerously," not simply mastering basic routines.

Let's Get Rid of Management

People
don't want
to be
managed.
They want
to be led.
Whoever heard
of a world
manager?
World leader,
yes.
Educational leader.
Political leader.
Religious leader.
Scout leader.
Community leader.
Labor leader.
Business leader.
They lead.
They don't manage.
The carrot
always wins
over the stick.
Ask your horse.
You can *lead* your
horse to water,
but you can't
manage him
to drink.
If you want to
manage somebody,
manage yourself.
Do that well
and you'll
be ready to
stop managing.
And start
leading.

Fig. 1. A message as published in the *Wall Street Journal* by United Technologies Corporation, Hartford, Connecticut 06101.

The "methodology" we used—if that's the proper word to apply, and we doubt it—was a combination of interviewing and observations. Like many fascinating (and fascinated) people, the ninety leaders had as many questions as answers. The "interviews" became more like exploratory dialogues and the so-called subjects became our coinvestigators. In most cases, the topic of leadership was discussed in three or four hours; in ten cases, we spent about five days with the leader (in two of those cases we actually lived with the leader, commuted to work with him, and got to know "the family" and the leader's staff and board members) in an attempt to learn about the organizational culture over which he presided.

The dialogues were "unstructured"; that is, they proceeded in an informal, rambling manner and were led only vaguely and intermittently by us. We went about these discussions much the way oil drillers go after oil. You chivvy around for the best position for the drill and keep probing and testing until you "hit." Then you stay there until it dries up. Then move on to another spot. There were only three questions asked of all leaders: "What are your strengths and weaknesses?" "Was there any particular experience or event in your life that influenced your management philosophy or style?" (There almost always was.) "What were the major decision points in your career and how do you feel about your choices now?" Those questions were the pivots around which the entire discussion revolved and they elicited rich, lively, and juicy responses. There's no other way to describe them.

Those interviewed included William Kieschnick, CEO of ARCO;* Ray Kroc of McDonald's fame; Franklin Murphy, chairman of Times-Mirror; Donald Seibert, chairman of JCPenney; John H. Johnson, publisher of *Ebony*; Donald Gevirtz, chairman of the Foothill Group; and James Rouse, chairman of Rouse Company. The public sector was much more varied: university presidents, the head of a major government agency (Harold Williams, former chairman of the Securities and Exchange Commission), coaches (John Robinson of the University of Southern California and Ray Meyer of DePaul University), orchestra conductors, and public interest leaders such as Vernon Jordan, former head of the Urban League. In addition, there was E. Robert Turner, former city manager of Cincinnati; William Donaldson, president of the Philadelphia Zoological Society; and Neil Armstrong, the first man on the moon, who personifies the genuine all-American hero.

It was a search for similarities in a wildly diverse group. Roughly half of the 60 CEOs were from *Fortune*'s top-200 list. The remainder were from smaller companies and enterprises. The median age (for the Corporate America group) was 56, the average income $400,000 (without "perks"). The average number of years with the company was 22.5 and the number of years as CEO was 8.5. Almost all were white males, reflecting the legacy of sexism and

---

*This title and affiliation, as well as those that follow, were those of the leaders at the time they were interviewed. Since that time, some of the leaders have moved on to other organizations or have retired.

racism in the corporate world.* Most had college degrees—25 percent with advanced degrees and about 40 percent with degrees in business—again proving the hypothesis that you don't have to have a business degree to succeed. In short, with one exception, there were no surprises, demographically, in the CEO group; as a group, they corresponded almost perfectly to the various profiles of corporate leadership in America.[1] The only surprise worth mentioning is that almost all were married to their first spouse. And not only that: They were also indefatigably enthusiastic about marriage as an institution.

Otherwise, there seemed to be no obvious patterns for their success. They were right-brained and left-brained, tall and short, fat and thin, articulate and inarticulate, assertive and retiring, dressed for success and dressed for failure, participative and autocratic. There were more variations than themes. Even their managerial styles were restlessly different. (One confided that, by nature, he believed in "participative fascism.") For those of us interested in pattern, in underlying themes, this group was frustratingly unruly. But they also gave testimony to the multifarious opportunities that are uniquely American.

THE FOUR STRATEGIES

However, determined to get our "conceptual arms" around the leadership issue, we vigilantly trolled

---

*There were six women and six black men in the group, but for reasons just stated, they weren't easy to come by. We had to make special efforts to identify them.

these disparate powers for uniformities, a process that eventually took about two years. And we did this much the way one decants wine or pans for gold, by continuously (and monotonously) going over the interviews and notes and trying out one concept to see how much of the data it could screen out and how much it could hold. Then another. And another. We looked to see if there were any kernels of truth about leadership—the marrow, if you will, of leadership behavior. Perhaps others would look elsewhere; for us, four major themes slowly developed, four areas of competency, four types of human handling skills, that all ninety of our leaders embodied:

- Strategy I: attention through vision
- Strategy II: meaning through communication
- Strategy III: trust through positioning
- Strategy IV: the deployment of self through (1) positive self-regard and (2) the Wallenda factor

Leadership seems to be the marshaling of skills possessed by a majority but used by a minority. But it's something that can be learned by anyone, taught to everyone, denied to no one.

Only a few will lead nations, but more will lead companies. Many more will lead departments or small groups. Those who aren't department heads will be supervisors. Those who follow on the assembly line may lead at the union hall. Like other complex skills, some people start out with more fully formed abilities than others. But what we determined is that the four "managements" can be learned, developed, and improved upon. And like fine wine, these competencies are the distilled essence of something much larger—peace, productivity, and perhaps freedom itself.

Strategy I:
Attention Through Vision

All men dream; but not equally.
Those who dream by night in the dusty
    recesses of their minds
Awake to find that it was vanity;
But the dreamers of day are dangerous men,
That they may act their dreams with open
    eyes to make it possible.

T. E. Lawrence

Management of attention through *vision* is the *creating of focus*. All ninety people interviewed had an *agenda*, an unparalleled concern with outcome. Leaders are the most results-oriented individuals in the world, and results get attention. Their visions or intentions are compelling and pull people toward them. Intensity coupled with commitment is magnetic. And these intense personalities do not have to coerce people to pay attention; they are so intent on what they are doing that, like a child completely absorbed with creating a sand castle in a sandbox, they draw others in.

Vision *grabs*. Initially it grabs the leader, and management of attention enables others also to get on the bandwagon. We visited Ray Kroc at "Hamburger U" in Elk Grove, Illinois, near Chicago, where McDonald's employees can get a "Bachelor of Hamburgerology with a minor in French fries." Kroc told the circumstances of his initial vision. He was already a tremendously successful paper cup manufacturer when he began manufacturing milkshake machines. He met the McDonald brothers, who owned a chain of milkshake parlors, and that collusion of cups and shakes set off the spark—a phenomenon we now know as McDonald's. When asked what leads to such serendipitous notions, Kroc answered, "I can't pretend to know what it is. Certainly it is not some divine vision. Perhaps it's a combination of your background, your instincts and your dreams. Whatever it was at that moment, I suppose I became an entrepreneur and decided to go for broke."

Another of the survey participants was Sergiu Comissioná, the renowned conductor of the Houston Symphony. For a long time he refused to be interviewed, which was remarkable in and of itself. He wouldn't respond to letters; he wouldn't respond to phone calls. After many months we were able to get in touch with two of his musicians. When asked what Comissioná was like, they answered, "Terrific." But when asked why, they wavered. Finally they said, "Because he doesn't waste our time."

That simple declarative sentence at first seemed insignificant. But when we finally watched him conduct and teach his master classes, we began to understand the full meaning of that phrase "he doesn't waste our time." It became clear that Comissioná transmits an unbridled clarity about what he wants from the players. He knows precisely and emphatically what he wants to hear at any given time. This fixation with and undeviating attention to outcome—some would call it an obsession—is only possible if one knows what he wants. And that can come only from vision or, as one member of Comissioná's orchestra referred to it, from "the maestro's tapestry of intentions."

There is a high, intense filament we noticed in our leaders—similar to Comissioná's passion about the "right" tone—and in any person impassioned with an idea. Sometimes it burns only within the range of their vision, and outside that range they can be as dull or interesting as anyone else. But this intensity is the battery for their attention. And attention is the first step to implementing or orchestrating a vision external to one's own actions.

An actress working on a set with one of our leaders, in this case a director, commented about him: "He reminds me of a child at play . . . very determined. . . . He says, like a child, 'I want this or I want that.' When he explains things, it is like a child who says, 'I want a castle built for me,' and he gets it." (Which brings to mind the composer Anton Bruckner, who, musing aloud to his fiancée, exclaimed, "But my dear, how can I find time to get married? I'm working on my Fourth Symphony.")

The visions these various leaders conveyed seemed to bring about a confidence on the part of the employees, a confidence that instilled in them a belief that they were capable of performing the necessary acts. These leaders were challengers, not coddlers. Edwin H. Land, founder of Polaroid, said: "The first thing you naturally do is teach the person to feel that the undertaking is manifestly important and nearly impossible. . . . That draws out the kind of drives that make people strong, that put you in pursuit intellectually."

Vision animates, inspirits, transforms purpose into action. Lincoln Kirstein, founder of the New York City Ballet and School, said: "My whole life has been trying to learn how things are done. What I love about the ballet is not that it looks pretty. It's the method in it. Ballet is about how to behave." And one of his associates said about him: "He has a power of concentration the likes of which I've never seen. He always knew what he wanted." (That's why it was also said about Kirstein that he never "wastes your time.") He said about his house: "Everything in this house is didactic and serves a purpose." Incidentally, his dress never varies: black suit, black socks, black tie, white shirt. Every day. "I long ago worked out that I would save a great deal of time if I forwent the particular choice of dress."

Incidentally, one of Kirstein's heroes, a namesake, is Abraham Lincoln, our sixteenth president. This choice of a hero dramatizes the significance of vision: "The superiority of Lincoln over all other states-men," he wrote, "lies in the limitless dimensions of a conscious self, its capacities and conditions of deployment. . . . In it, we see the Lincolnian self, capable of delay, double-talk, maneuver, hesitancy, compromise, in order that one prime aim of his own era be effected: preservation of Federal union."

Listen to that pneumatic sense of purpose that comes through in Kirstein's admiration of President Lincoln—"preservation of Federal union." At all costs. It's worth sacrifice, even dissembling for. But even less vaunted visions seem to hold the same value for the leaders, whether the vision is instant photography or fast-food restaurants. These leaders recall a character from Shaw's *Man and Superman*:[2]

> This is the true joy in life, the being used for a purpose recognized by yourself as a mighty one; the being a force of nature instead of a feverish selfish little clod of ailments and grievances complaining that the world will not devote itself to making you happy.
>
> I want to be thoroughly used up when I die, for the harder I work the more I live. I rejoice in life for its own sake. Life is no "brief candle" to me. It is a sort of splendid torch which I have got hold of for the moment, and I want to make it burn as brightly as possible before handing it on to future generations.

But leadership is also a transaction, a transaction between leaders and followers. Neither could exist without the other. There has to be resonance, a connection between them. So what we discovered is that leaders also *pay attention* as well as catch it. Even though Comissioná and Land, Kroc and Kirstein are commanding figures, the interaction between the leader and the led is tacitly far more complicated than the simple command; they bring out the best in each other. Later on we'll go into this in far more detail. But for now we can say that the new leadership under discussion is not arbitrary or unilateral but rather an impressive and subtle sweeping back and forth of energy, whether between maestro and players or CEO and staff. The transaction creates unity. Conductor and orchestra as one. Coach and team. Leader and organization as one. And that unified focus is the management of attention through vision.

Strategy II:
Meaning Through Communication

If you can dream it, you can do it.
Walt Disney

This quote from Disney figures high on a sign at Epcot in Orlando, Florida. While it does beckon the Don Quixote in us all, the idea is incomplete. Believing in one's dreams is not enough. There are a lot of intoxicating visions and a lot of noble intentions. Many people have rich and deeply textured agendas, but without communication nothing will be realized. Success requires the capacity to relate a compelling image of a desired state of affairs—the kind of image that induces enthusiasm and commitment in others.

How do you capture imaginations? How do you communicate visions? How do you get people aligned behind the organization's overarching goals? How do you get an audience to recognize and accept an idea? Workers have to recognize and get behind something of established identity. The management of meaning, mastery of communication, is inseparable from effective leadership.

Interestingly, while many of the ninety leaders interviewed were tremendously articulate, there were those individuals who turned out to be less so. However, wordlessness did not hamper their communications style. One great entrepreneur from Buffalo is Bill Moog, founder and head of Moog, Inc., a manufacturer of patented and essential aircraft engine parts. Moog remained silent for long periods of time during the interview. He seemed deeply inside his own thoughts, and yet the intensity of his appearance was commanding. This concentration is characterized by a claim he makes to having once remained awake for six months deliberating over a problem. His wife, who happened to be with him during the interview, shook her head and said, "Bill *didn't* go to bed for six months. He occasionally slept during meetings, but he never actually did the thing of 'going to sleep.'" There's no better way to describe a conversation with Moog than to simply quote from one. Here's a classic excerpt:

Q. How *do* you communicate . . . you, yourself? Because you appear to be so taciturn. . . .

A. Sometimes we don't communicate at all. A period of six months might elapse before we have any conversation one way or the other.

Q. Really?

A. But somehow or the other the construct always seems to get across. We know what's happening . . . know what's going on. Pretty unusual. (*Long pause*) Well . . . there's an element of trust and confidence, as I said, and there's enough continuity, so that they know what to expect. My patterns. . . . (*Long pause*)

Q. But isn't your "quietness" a drawback, especially for new employees?

A. Maybe. I don't know. Seems to me that when I feel strongly about something, people know it. I'm not sure how or why. I do draw pictures from time to time and send those out or else I build a model. When we decentralized a couple of years ago, I sent around a mock-up of the way I wanted our organization to look. Drew it on graph paper . . . people seemed to get it. Made the move, from one kind of organization to another—including some physical moves— without losing one day's productivity. . . .

So, it seems, at work, Moog is accustomed to presenting models or drawings to get his meanings across. His employees understand his intention through these "concretized" ideas. A lot of our leaders had a penchant for metaphor if not for models. Comparison, analogy, bring subjects to life. It is, for instance, clearer to speak of an acre as roughly the size of a football field than to identify it as 4,840 square yards.

Before directing *Ordinary People*, Robert Redford knew relatively little about cinematography. The first morning on the set, he took the six cinematographers aside and played them Pachelbel's Canon in D, the gorgeous music that opens the movie. Redford said to them, "I want you to listen to this, and I want you to think about what a suburban scene would look like if it corresponded to the music." What he was doing, without realizing it, is what psychologists call synesthesia, or transforming one sense to another rather as Disney did in *Fantasia*.

Former President Reagan, likewise, had a flair for reifying abstract topics with experiential references. His first budget message was a sort of masterpiece in that he objectified $1 trillion by comparing it to the Empire State Building. His ability to express his ideas graphically was a major policy-wielding device. According to an ABC poll, support for the U.S. invasion of Grenada *doubled* immediately after Reagan's explanatory speech.

However it is done, effective communication is essential to rallying supporters, especially when the leader's vision calls for great change or sacrifice. A half century ago, Roosevelt and Churchill were the great communicators, and in more recent times, Nelson Mandela, Margaret Thatcher and Yitzhak Rabin were among the leaders who reshaped their societies through their extraordinary persuasive abilities.

Conversely, Jimmy Carter was unimpressive in his ability to communicate, which greatly hampered his rallying power. Ironically, Carter was probably one of the best-informed presidents since Woodrow Wilson. However, it isn't just information or facts—which can be received as "info-glut"—it's the *form* of presentation, the overall meaning. President Carter's intentions were there, but the forms were vague. One of the people interviewed, a cabinet officer and loyal Democrat appointed by Carter, remarked how difficult it had been to work for him because she never knew what he stood for. As she talked about Jimmy Carter, she conjured a beautiful metaphor of her own: "Working for him was like looking at the wrong side of a tapestry—blurry and indistinct."

This reliance on "someone" to define reality in a group is well illustrated by a favorite anecdote, a baseball story. It takes place in the last inning of a very key game, playoff for the pennant, with 3-2 on the batter. The final pitch comes over, the umpire hesitates a split second. The batter angrily turns around and says, "Well, what was it?" The umpire then replies, "It ain't nothin' 'til I call it."

When Frank Dale took over the *Los Angeles Herald-Examiner*, Los Angeles's afternoon newspaper, it was just ending a bloody ten-year-old strike. The building was barricaded and had not been open in eight years. Dale, the new president and publisher, had to go in through the back to greet his irksome staff.

Listen to Dale's words:

I started the pattern the very first hour I was there. A new manager. . . . It so happened that the front door of the building was barricaded. It had not been open in eight years. I had to walk through the back door, have my fingerprints taken, my picture taken: "Welcome aboard, boss!" I went to the newsroom within the first hour and asked the people who were working to come and gather around me so I could introduce myself—I had no one else. . . .

Q. You mean, you couldn't walk through the front door?

A. That's right. The lobby had been barricaded for over eight years. There was tremendous strife, people were killed, employees were killed and indeed, it was eventually some employees who had never been unionized or related to any union who simply said to each other over a beer one night: "We gotta quit shooting each other." And so, on a peace platform, they got the employees to vote for a settlement and eventually got the right to bargain and that was done. I called the people on duty at the time around the desk in an informal setting—I had no one to introduce me. . . . I did it myself so that I would be right there and without any forethought at all I said, "Maybe the first thing we ought to do is open up the front door." Everybody stood up and cheered. Grown men and women cried. That was a symbol, you see, that barricade was a symbol of defeat, of siege. And "let the sunshine in" was what I was saying. . . . And then I attempted to introduce myself again, thanked them for preserving the opportunity that I had been asked to take advantage of. Which is really what they did— when I let the sunshine in. . . .

Once the *Herald-Examiner* was operational, Dale developed a kind of missile idea as a metaphor for a campaign to increase circulation. There were posters on virtually every wall and all bulletin boards showing the *Herald-Examiner* (as a spaceship) catching up with its powerful morning rival, the *Los Angeles Times*. In keeping with this "taking off" image, his office chair is equipped with an airplane seat belt, which to this day he still patiently fastens.

A number of lessons can be drawn from the experiences of our ninety leaders. First, and perhaps most important, is that *all* organizations depend on the existence of shared meanings and interpretations of reality, which facilitate coordinated action. The actions and symbols of leadership frame and mobilize meaning. Leaders articulate and define what has previously remained implicit or unsaid; then they invent images, metaphors, and models that provide a focus for new attention. By so doing, they consolidate or challenge prevailing wisdom. In short, an *essential* factor in leadership is the capacity to influence and *organize meaning* for the members of the organization. (We'll have more to say about this in the chapter on Strategy II.)

The second thing to keep in mind is that the style and means by which leaders convey and shape meaning varies enormously, from the visual exercises of a Redford to the models of a Moog, from the symbolic "letting the sunshine in" of a Frank Dale to the exquisite verbal imagery of an Edwin Land. Despite the variations in style, however—whether verbal or nonverbal, whether through words or music—every successful leader is aware that an organization is based on a set of shared meanings that define roles and authority. He or she is also aware that a pivotal responsibility is to communicate the blueprint which shapes and interprets situations so that the actions of employees are guided by common interpretations of reality.

Finally, what we mean by "meaning" goes far beyond what is usually meant by "communication." For one thing, it has very little to do with "facts" or even "knowing." Facts and knowing have to do with technique, with methodology, with "knowing how to do things." That's useful, even necessary, and undeniably occupies a useful place in today's scheme of things. But thinking is emphatically closer to what we mean by "meaning" than knowing is. Thinking prepares one for what is to be done, what ought to be done. Thinking, though it may be unsettling and dangerous to the established order, is constructive: it challenges old conventions by suggesting new directions, new visions. To depend on facts, without thinking, may seem safe and secure, but in the long run it is dangerously unconstructive because it has nothing to say about *directions*. The distinctive role of leadership (in a volatile environment especially) is the quest for "know-why" ahead of "know-how." And this distinction illustrates, once again, one of the key differences between leaders and managers.

Let's stay with this for a while longer, since the distinction we're attempting to draw has implications that go well beyond leadership and into other even more abstruse matters, such as creativity and aesthetics. Managers, for the most part, deal with a mental process known as problem solving. Problem solving involves a problem, a method, and a solution that follows from the problem and method. A creative mental process occurs when neither the problem nor the method, let alone the solution, exists as a known entity. Creativity involves a "discovered problem," one that needs to be worked out from beginning to end. The highest form of discovery always requires *problem finding*. This is very like the identification of a new direction or vision for an organization. This is the difference we noted earlier between leaders and managers; it is the difference between routine problem solvers and problem finders.

But how does one *know* whether a discovered problem or a creative idea is valuable? How does one evaluate that? If one decides, for example, to go from Los Angeles to Aspen by the shortest route, normal problem solving can easily solve that by finding the itinerary that best conforms to the parameters of the problem. But suppose one asked: Is it a good idea to go from Los Angeles to Aspen by the shortest route? Then reasoning and logic would have a hard time coming up with an answer. Cognitive criteria are not sufficient to evaluate creative solutions. But then how are they recognized? Why do constituents align behind one solution, direction or vision and not another?

The best answer we can give to that venerable question is that the acceptance of a vision—or any new idea, for that matter—requires that the employees (or any audience) be willing to pay attention to the would-be creative contribution. However, we must quickly add that the acceptance of a new idea is never determined solely by the quality of that idea. Even the "best" ideas are only as good as their ability to attract attention in the social environment. The conditions of that environment—organizations in this case—are inherently unpredictable: They can kill a good idea just as easily as a bad one.

The main clue is that leadership creates a new audience for its ideas because it alters the shape of understanding by transmitting information in such a way that it "fixes" and secures tradition. Leadership, by communicating meaning, creates a *commonwealth of learning*, and that, in turn, is what effective organizations are.

What we see and experience in today's organizational landscape are cumbersome bureaucracies that more often than not betray the *mismanagement* of meaning. A "great idea" is hatched. Responsibility is delegated. Then it is delegated again. Then it is redelegated. By the time the "great idea" is carried out it is like a thalidomide child with no parents—certainly not what the leaders intended or anticipated. This "Pinocchio effect" is the bane of many creators who, like Geppetto, are confronted with distended, distorted versions of original plans. Lack of clarity makes bureaucracies little more than mechanisms for the evasion of responsibility and guilt.

Communication creates meaning for people. Or should. It's the only way any group, small or large, can become aligned behind the overarching goals of an organization. Getting the message across unequivocally at every level is an absolute key. Basically it is what the creative process is all about and what, once again, separates the managers from the leaders.

Strategy III:
Trust Through Positioning

Nothing worthwhile can be accomplished without determination. In the early days of nuclear power, for example,
getting approval to build the first nuclear submarine—the
Nautilus—was almost as difficult as designing and building it. Good ideas are not adopted automatically. They
must be driven into practice with courageous patience.

Admiral Hyman Rickover

Trust is the lubrication that makes it possible for
organizations to work. It's hard to imagine an *organization* without some semblance of trust operating
somehow, somewhere. An organization without trust
is more than an anomaly, it's a misnomer, a dim crea-
ture of Kafka's imagination. Trust implies account-
ability, predictability, reliability. It's what sells products and keeps organizations humming. Trust is the
glue that maintains organizational integrity.

Like leadership, trust is hard to describe, let alone
define. We know when it's present and we know
when it's not, and we cannot say much more about it
except for its essentiality and that it is based on predictability. The truth is that we trust people who are
predictable, whose positions are known and who
keep at it; leaders who are trusted make themselves
known, make their positions clear.

Theodore Friend III, the past president of Swarthmore College, told us how he defined "leadership":

Leadership is heading into the wind with such
knowledge of oneself and such collaborative

energy as to move others to wish to follow. *The angle into the wind is less important than choosing one and sticking reasonably to it,* which reasonability includes willingness to be borne by friendly currents. [Emphasis added.]

Followers do not collect to exhortation, but adhere from example. In action and in articulation, leading requires that one know where one is taking oneself: from the being that has been to the one that wishes to be, despite ambiguities, and against the odds that inhere in ideals.

Note Dr. Friend's emphasis on *position*, on knowing what is right and necessary. Our leaders, in a variety of ways, echoed that same principle. Leaders are reliable and tirelessly persistent.

This ceaseless positioning was at the core of Martin Luther King Jr.'s human rights movement and fueled Susan B. Anthony's women's vote crusade. Exceptional people have made continual sacrifices, sometimes even facing death for causes in which they believed, because they chose an angle and stuck reasonably to it. Ultimately, it is this relentless dedication that engages *trust*.

One of the first things Ray Kroc did when we entered his office was to remove from the wall an elaborately framed statement composed by Calvin Coolidge. It was his favorite inspirational message and is worth reprinting here:

Nothing in the world can take the place of persistence.

Talent will not; nothing is more common than unsuccessful men with great talent.

Genius will not; unrewarded genius is almost a proverb.

Education will not; the world is full of educated derelicts.

Persistence, determination alone are omnipotent.

Every executive office we visited at McDonald's headquarters had that message framed and positioned so that no visitor could miss it.

To sum up, what we've been getting at thus far is that positioning is the set of actions necessary to implement the vision of the leader. If vision is the idea, then positioning is the niche the leader establishes. For this niche to be achieved, the leader must be the epitome not only of clarity (which the previous section emphasized) but of constancy, of reliability. Through establishing the position—and, more important, staying the course—leadership establishes trust.

Indeed, the most common statement made about the ninety leaders by their board members and staff members was that they were "all of a piece." Leaders acquire and wear their visions like clothes. Accordingly, they seem to enroll themselves (and then others) in the belief of their ideals as attainable, and their behavior exemplifies the ideals in action.

Nelson Mandela is perhaps the most stellar model since Mahatma Gandhi of a leader who radically transformed his nation by serving as a role model for his followers and persistently living his ideals. From the time he joined the African National Congress (ANC) as a young man in 1944, through twenty years of bitter political struggle followed by twenty-six years in prison, he never wavered in his drive to eliminate apartheid in South Africa. His constancy paid off in 1990 when he led the ANC through tortuous negotiations with the government of F. W. de Klerk to effect a peaceful transition to a multiracial government. The Nobel Peace Prize in 1993 and election to the presidency of South Africa shortly thereafter were tributes of a grateful world and nation to his remarkable tenacity as a leader.

Former President Reagan, whose motto "stay the course" turned out to be extremely winning, was a symphony in self-image maintenance and constancy. Time and time again, he hot-footed it over a bed of controversy and catastrophe and still managed to sustain his decorous bravado. While various members of his staff squabbled, he remained stalwart, intact. His assumption of responsibility for the Marines' susceptibility in Beirut was perceived as heroic. His congratulation of the Reverend Jesse Jackson ("Can't argue with success," he said) was "good sportsmanship." Even blatant manipulation of public opinion, as in his support of the Pentagon's press ban in Grenada, was received with overwhelming approval (except by the press). While his actions were arguably "the right thing," Reagan understood that it's not necessarily the direction (the angle you take) that counts, but sticking reasonably to the direction you choose.

All leadership requires this constancy. Alfred P. Sloan provides one of the best examples of this. When he came to General Motors, it was a hodge-podge with no established policy. He wrote: "The spacing of our product line of ten cars in seven lines in early 1921 reveals its irrationality. . . . Some kind of rationality was called for."[3] Sloan made his reputation and transformed General Motors into a great firm by positioning GM in the marketplace. He did this by reducing the entire product line to just six pricing steps and creating new cars in the low-priced $600 to $900 categories. Without question, Sloan felt that positioning GM properly in its environment was one of his most important responsibilities as leader. Even though they were unaware of it, the leaders we interviewed acted on an old Chinese proverb: "If we don't change our direction, we're likely to end up where we're headed."

There are two terribly important reasons for stressing *the management of trust through positioning*. The first has to do with "organizational integrity." We have observed that an effective organizational structure can be compared to healthy individuals and is something observed in them; in fact, it is analogous to a healthy identity. More technically, we can assume that an organization possesses a healthy structure when it has a clear sense of what it is and what it is to do. That's another way of saying "choosing a direction and staying with it." It is also a way of defining organizational integrity, and it is a handle by which leaders can better understand and shape their culture.

But organizational integrity is more easily defined than achieved. Part of the problem is the lack of understanding of the various substructures that all organizations, no matter how small, contain. One block to our understanding is perpetuated by the myth of organization as monolith, a myth reinforced almost daily by the media and the temptation of simplicity. The myth is not only grossly inaccurate but dangerous as well. When the evening paper, for example, announces that the Defense Department or the University of California or IBM (or any corporate body, for that matter) will pursue this or that course of action, the said action is typically consigned to a single, composite body, *the* administration. This "administration"—whose parts vibrate in harmony and whose acts, because we are denied a look at the human drama that leads up to them, take on an air of superhuman detachment—is as mythical as the griffin. Into every step taken by *the* administration goes a complicated pattern of meetings, disagreements, conversations, personalities, emotions, and missed connections. This very human process is bureaucratic politics. A parallel process is responsible for our foreign policy, the quality of our public schools, the scope and treatment of the news that the media choose to deliver to us each day.

Our perceptions of organizational decision making, based on such reports and other stimuli, tend to emphasize the *product* of decision making, never (or rarely) the *process*. The result, of course, is false; at times, destructively so. Those elements of chance, ignorance, stupidity, recklessness and amiable confusion are simply not reckoned with; they are selectively ignored, it seems. Thus, the public rarely sees the hundreds of small tableaux, the little dramas, that result in a policy statement or a bit of strategy. It sees only the move or hears only the statement, and it not unreasonably assumes that such an action is the result of a dispassionate, almost mechanical process in which problems are perceived, alternative solutions weighed, and rational decisions made. Given human nature, that is almost never the case.

In order for an organization to have integrity, it must have an identity—that is, a sense of who it is and what it is to do. Perhaps an analogy taken from personality theory will illustrate as well as foreshadow the point. Every person is a summation of various "selves." If those units of the person are not in communication, then the person cannot maintain valid communications with others. The problem of integrity, which is central to much of the contemporary literature in the mental health field, can be examined in organizations by understanding the various "organizational selves" or structures that exist.

Every organization incorporates four concepts of organization; these are often at odds with one another, or they exist in some strained coherence. There is the *manifest* organization, the one that is seen on the "organizational chart" and is either formally displayed or hidden. It masks as much reality as it is alleged to portray. Then there is the *assumed* organization, the one that individuals perceive actually to be existing. On occasion, we have asked employees to draw their view of the way things work in order to capture their perceptions. The discrepancy between their view and the official view—the manifest organization—is always dramatic. Thirdly, there is the *extant* organization, or the situation as revealed through systematic investigation—say, by an organizational consultant who attempts to achieve an "objective look." Finally, there is the *requisite* organization, or the organization as it would look if it were in accord with the reality of the situation within which it exists.*

The ideal but never realized situation is that in which the manifest, the assumed, the extant, and the requisite are aligned as closely as possible with each other. Wherever these four organizational concepts are in contradiction, the organizational culture is such that its identity is confused and integrity difficult to achieve.

Another useful analogy to mental health shows up in this discussion. Many, if not all, psychotherapeutic schools base their notions of mental health on the degree to which the individual brings into harmony the various "selves" that make up his or her personality. The healthy person will be much the same person as others know him or her to be.

Virtually the same criterion can be used to establish organizational integrity—that is, the degree to

---

*These ideas were originally expressed by Elliott Jaques, M.D.

which the organization maintains harmony and knowledge about and among the manifest, assumed, extant, and requisite concepts. It is not necessary that all four concepts be identical. Rather, all four types should be recognized and allowance made for all tensions created by imbalances. It is doubtful that an organization can (or even should) achieve total congruence. The important factor is recognition, a heightened consciousness of the confusions and contradictions. And this cannot be realized without positioning.

The second reason behind the significance of positioning has to do with "staying the course": constancy. As we've said throughout, effective leadership takes risks—it innovates, challenges, and changes the basic metabolism of the organizational culture. This form of leadership requires what Admiral Rickover alluded to in the statement quoted earlier as "courageous patience." In practice, this means "keeping at it" and "at it" and, once again, "at it." Innovation—any new idea—by definition will not be accepted at first, no matter how sensational the idea may be. If everyone embraced the innovation, it would be difficult to take it seriously—as an innovation. Innovation causes resistance to stiffen, defense to set in, opposition to form. And any new idea looks either foolish or impractical or unfeasible—at first. It takes repeated attempts, endless demonstrations, monotonous rehearsals before innovation can be accepted and internalized by any organization. This requires staying power and, yes, "courageous patience."

One of our nation's largest food-processing companies repeatedly failed in its attempt to develop a successful piecrust mix. Test market after test market proved to be a disaster. Each year the lab came up with a new recipe that would not fail, and each year it did flop—literally—at least in the important test markets. Executives got so bored and burned with the annual fizzles that they started to refer to it as Project Lazarus, since it seemed to be resurrected from the dead so many times. Now, only because the company kept at it and finally came up with a winner, this piecrust mix is its leading product both in sales and profits.

As Woody Allen once said, "eighty percent of success is just showing up." The same appears to hold true for organizations and their leaders who have learned to manage trust through positioning.

It may be appropriate to conclude this section with a charming and inspirational poem by Don Marquis, which reflects the spirit of positioning (and "courageous patience"):

The Lesson of the Moth[4]

I was talking to a moth the other evening.
He was trying to break into an electric light bulb and
    fry himself on the wire.
"Why do you fellows pull this stunt?" I asked him.
"Because it is a conventional thing for moths?
Or why, if that had been an uncovered candle, instead
    of an electric light bulb,

You would now be a small, unsightly cinder.
Have you no sense?"
"Plenty of it," he answered, "but at times we get tired
    of using it.
We get bored with the routine and crave beauty and
    excitement.
Fire is beautiful and we know that if we get too close it
    will kill us,
But what does it matter?
It is better to be happy for a moment and be burned up
    with beauty
Than to live a long time and be bored all the while.
So we wad all our life up into one little roll,
And then we shoot the roll.
That's what life is for.
It is better to be a part of beauty for one instant
And then cease to exist,
Than to exist forever and never be a part of beauty.
Our attitude toward life is
Come easy, go easy.
We're like human beings used to be before they became
    too civilized to enjoy themselves."
And before I could argue him out of his philosophy,
He went and immolated himself on a patented cigar
    lighter.
I do not agree with him.
Myself, I would rather have half the happiness
And twice the longevity.
But at the same time,
I wished there was something I wanted
As badly as he wanted to fry himself.

Strategy IV:
The Deployment of Self Through
Positive Self-Regard

When Yen Ho was about to take up his duties as tutor to
the heir of Ling, Duke of Wei, he went to Ch'u Po Yu for
advice. "I have to deal," he said, "with a man of depraved
and murderous disposition. . . . How is one to deal with a
man of this sort?" "I am glad," said Ch'u Po Yu, "that you
asked this question. . . . The first thing you must do is not
to improve him, but to improve yourself."

Taoist story of ancient China

My intention always has been to arrive at human contact
without enforcing authority. A musician, after all, is not a
military officer. What matters most is human contact. The
great mystery of music making requires real friendship
among those who work together. Every member of the
orchestra knows I am with him and her in my heart.

Carlo Maria Giulini
Conductor, Los Angeles Philharmonic

These two quotes both frame and illustrate the fact
that leadership is an essentially human business.
Both universities and corporations seriously miss the
point with their overemphasis on formal quantitative tools, unambiguous problems, and ridiculously
oversimplified "human relations" cases. What we
have found is that the higher the rank, the more
interpersonal and human the undertaking. Our top
executives spent roughly 90 percent of their time
with others and virtually the same percentage of
their time concerned with the messiness of people
problems. Our study of effective leaders strongly suggested that a key factor was the *creative deployment*

of self. What that's all about will be taken up in the remainder of this chapter.

The management of self is critical. Without it, leaders may do more harm than good. Like incompetent physicians, incompetent managers can make people sicker and less vital. The word "iatrogenic" may be useful to employ in this respect. It refers to illnesses caused by doctors and hospitals as side effects of medical intervention. Managers, too, can cause as well as cure problems.

Fred Friendly, former president of CBS News, provides an excellent example of this. He is "hyper" and beset with visions, which he pelts at unnerved listeners. When once asked if he'd ever had a nervous breakdown, he replied, "No, but I'm a carrier." So though we've always known that some managers give themselves heart attacks and other self-induced problems, what's even more forbidding is that they can also infect their employees with the same. That's what we mean by "iatrogenic." Which leads us to the inexorable conclusion that effective leadership is no less noble or base than the creative (and healthy) use of one's self.

This creative deployment of self makes leading, as we noted, a deeply personal business. It's what we're calling, more out of convenience than precision, positive self-regard. We learned the meaning of this phrase from responses to one of our three standard questions: "What are your major strengths and weaknesses?" For the most part, the leaders emphasized their strengths and tended to soft-pedal or minimize their weaknesses. Which is not to say that they weren't aware of personal weaknesses but rather that they didn't harp on them. One of the CEOs interviewed, Dr. Franklin Murphy, former chairman of the Times-Mirror publishing empire and the embodiment of positive self-regard, said he had no "second thoughts" about turning down four opportunities to join the president's cabinet. "I just didn't think I'd be good at that sort of thing," he said.

It may be easier to say what positive self-regard isn't than what it is. To begin with, it is not a crowing self-importance or egoistic self-centeredness that we have in mind. Nor is it what's ordinarily meant by a "narcissistic character." There was no trace of self-worship or cockiness in our leaders.

But they know their worth. They trust themselves without letting their egos or images get in the way. One leader put it in terms of self-respect. She said,

> To have self-respect is everything. Without it, we are nothing but unwilling slaves, at everybody's mercy, especially those we fear or hold in contempt. . . . You think, "Well, no job is good enough; after all, if they want me, hired me, how could they (or the job) be any good?" Groucho Marx's greatest line says it all for those without self-respect, "I wouldn't join any club that would have me as a member." They choke on self-reproach. For them, every encounter demands too much and receives too little. Every unanswered letter becomes a monument to their own sloth, an epitaph to their guilt. Without self-respect, we give ourselves away and make the ultimate sacrifice: sell *ourselves* out!

Recognizing strengths and compensating for weaknesses represent the first step in achieving positive self-regard. The leaders in our study seemed to know what they were good at from an early age. John Korty, the producer, was making and distributing movies during his junior high school years in Ohio. Claire Townsend was publishing articles in her teens. Conductor James Levine made mature conductors nervous by the time he was five by keeping time with the score at his side while seated in the first row of the concert hall. There was no doubt in Andrew Grove's mind that he was mechanically precocious, and he knew that he wanted to "go into engineering" at an early age. Most of our leaders knew, early on in their lives, that they were good with people and that when they were in leadership roles they were successful.

So the first thing is the ability to recognize strengths and compensate for weaknesses. The *second element in positive self-regard is the nurturing of skills with discipline*—that is, to keep working on and developing one's talents. Many, though by no means all, of the leaders were athletes or athletic and were eager to get feedback and all manner of data about their performance. Like athletes, they regularly set higher goals and objectives for themselves, based on past performances. As Don Gevirtz, U.S. Ambassador to Fiji and former chairman of the Foothill Group, a lending institution, put it: "After the first million, I knew we could triple that in less than a year." Before Intel reached a $1 billion sales figure, its president, Andrew Grove, raised the goal to $1½ billion (that was in '94!). Howard Schultz, chairman and CEO of

Starbucks, intends to grow his outlets from 1,000 now to 2,000 by the end of this millennium.

But it's not the profit and loss or return on investment that we're primarily referring to. It's the capacity to develop and improve their skills that distinguished leaders from followers. They seemed to be responsible for their own evolution and even could appropriately be called "self-evolvers."

It should also be said that while there is no substitute for achievement, leaders need not be exceptional in every way. But limitations cannot be ignored. A trait that begins as little more than a personal hang-up can become tragic through repetition, so effective leaders learn to compensate for their imperfections before they become perilous. Deficiencies can actually be used to broaden the leadership base. One of the best examples of this is Will Clarkson who, when interviewed, was the chairman and CEO of Graphic Controls, Inc. Sensing, quite correctly, that his skills were based on his high-tech talents and not on human relations—as he put it, "I'm a 'things guy,' not a 'people guy'"—he started to attend human relations seminars and hired a consultant who could help him with his "people skills." After two years of that, he began a series of seminars on interpersonal and communications skills, which he took the time to teach himself. He became a superbly balanced leader.

Typically, effective CEOs either build a staff that covers and compensates for their perceived weakness or they do not take the job. Which leads to the third aspect of positive self-regard, *the capacity to discern the fit* between one's perceived skills and what the job requires. Very like Franklin Murphy who had "no second thoughts" in turning down a high government post.

Conventional wisdom often (and incorrectly) consigns to good timing what we attribute to this third element of positive self-regard, the fit between personal strengths and organizational requirements. What actually happens—and we learned this from reviewing in detail the career trajectories of the ninety leaders—is that they seemed to "know" when a particular job would fully exploit their strengths and when their unique qualities were no longer relevant (or could even be detrimental) for the organization. They seemed to know intuitively, to quote the country and western singer Kenny Rogers, "when to hold and when to fold." Their so-called good timing was more dependent on their capacity to discern the fit of strengths to needs than anything else.

An instructive way of looking at strengths and weaknesses is as "raw ingredients," or media necessary to an artistic plan. An aspiring individual works diligently with all personal characteristics and potentialities, including his or her shortcomings, until everything appears as a work of art which, as one of the ninety said, "delights the eye." The end result is a state of self-satisfaction and a fertile integrity that can conceive and carry out great visions.

We can sum up what we mean by positive self-regard. It consists of three major components: knowledge of one's strengths, the capacity to nurture and develop those strengths and the ability to discern the fit between one's strengths and weaknesses and the organization's needs. Another way of thinking about positive self-regard as it specifically relates to work and jobs is this: Individuals who possess it are good at their jobs; they have the requisite skills. They enjoy their work; it satisfies their basic needs and motives. And, finally, they are proud of their work; it reflects their value system.

The most astonishing *result* of positive self-regard came as something of a surprise to us, though in retrospect, we should have perhaps foreseen its most stunning effect. What we observed was that our ninety leaders induced (stemming from their own self-regard) positive *other*-regard in their employees. And this turns out to be a pivotal factor in their capacity to lead. Irwin Federman, former president and CEO of Monolithic Memories, illustrates this brilliantly in the following quote:

> If you think about it, people love others not for who they are, but for how they make us feel. We willingly follow others for much the same reason. It makes us feel good to do so. Now, we also follow platoon sergeants, self-centered geniuses, demanding spouses, bosses of various persuasions and others, for a variety of reasons as well. But none of those reasons involves that person's leadership qualities. In order to *willingly* accept the direction of another individual, it *must* feel good to do so. This business of making another person feel good in the unspectacular course of his daily comings and goings is, in my view, the very essence of leadership.

Another interesting illustration of the same point but pitched in a slightly different way came from an interview with James Rouse, the famous city planner and developer. When he was dissatisfied with the looks of some housing in his Columbia, Maryland, project, he tried to influence the next design by nagging and correcting his team of architects. He got nowhere. Then he decided to stop "correcting them" and tried to influence them by sending them to look at the world's best, demonstrating what he wanted, *what he was for.* Inspired by Rouse's vision, the architects went on to create some of the most eye-catching and functional housing in the country. What that illustrates is that the self-regard of leaders is *contagious.*

Two more examples: In the early days of Polaroid, Edwin Land continually inspired his team to "achieve the impossible." Land's compelling positive self-regard convinced his managers that they couldn't fail. When William Hewitt took over John Deere and Company in the mid-1950s, he turned a sleepy, old-line farm implements firm into a leader among modern multinational corporations. His secret: always asking, "Can't we do this a little better?" And the employees rose to the occasion. As one long-time Deere employee put it, "Hewitt made us learn how good we were."

Leaders with positive self-regard rarely, if ever, have to rely on criticism or negative sanctions, whether they lead a large multinational company, a symphony orchestra, or a football team. Coach John Robinson told us that he *never* criticizes his players until they're convinced of his *unconditional* confidence in their abilities. *After* that's achieved, he might say (if he does spot something that can help a player), "Look, what you're doing is 99 percent terrific, but there is that 1 percent factor that could make a difference. Let's work on that." When he was coach at USC, he told Marcus Allen, then a junior and later to become one of NFL's greatest running backs, something like that—but only after two years of building Allen's confidence.

Irwin Federman, quoted above, seems to say it all in a few cogent sentences:

> Our individual potential is a direct derivative of our self-esteem. Which means we feel good about ourselves. If we come to regard ourselves more highly, then we come to expect more of ourselves.... This growth process results in more aggressive goals, greater expectations and hence more impressive achievements. If you believe what I'm saying, you cannot help but come to the conclusions that those you have followed passionately, gladly, zealously—have made *you* feel like *somebody*. It was not merely because they had the job, or the power ... it somehow made you feel terrific to be around them.

Positive self-regard seems to exert its force by creating in others a sense of confidence and high expectations, not very different from the fabled Pygmalion effect. When Ian McGregor took over the chairmanship of the British Steel Corporation, his first order of business was to restore the morale of middle management. "I've always worked on the theory," he said, "that it's very important for the top person in an organization to figure out how to motivate." He couldn't offer his executives the financial rewards customary in money-making companies, but he could provide motivation by building up their independence and confidence. "People begin to feel they manage a piece of the business," he said. "They have greater opportunity to show their capabilities."

Positive self-regard is related to maturity, but we'd prefer the phrase "emotional wisdom" to "maturity." Maturity sounds too much like the point where one outgrows childish behavior. But our leaders seemed to retain many of the positive characteristics of the child: enthusiasm for people, spontaneity, imagination and an unlimited capacity to learn new behavior. Emotional wisdom, as we've come to understand it, reflects itself in the way people relate to others. In the case of our ninety leaders, they used five key skills:

1. The ability to accept people as they are, not as you would like them to be. In a way, this can be seen as the height of wisdom—to "enter the skin" of someone else, to understand what other people are like on *their* terms, rather than judging them.

2. The capacity to approach relationships and problems in terms of the present rather than the past. Certainly it is true that we can learn from past mistakes. But using the present as a takeoff point for trying to make fewer mistakes

seemed to be more productive for our leaders—
and certainly was more psychologically sound
than rehashing things that are over.

3. The ability to treat those who are close to you
with the same courteous attention that you
extend to strangers and casual acquaintances.
The need for this skill is often most obvious—
and lacking—in our relationships with our
own families. But it is equally important at
work. We tend to take for granted those to
whom we are closest. Often we get so accustomed to seeing them and hearing from them
that we lose our ability to listen to what they
are really saying or to appreciate the quality—
good or bad—of what they are doing. Personal
feelings of friendship or hostility or simple
indifference interfere.

There are two aspects to this problem of
overfamiliarity. The first is that of not hearing
what is being said: selective deafness leads to
misunderstandings, misconceptions, mistakes.
The second is the matter of feedback we fail to
provide to indicate our attentiveness.

4. The ability to trust others, even if the risk
seems great. A withholding of trust is often
necessary for self-protection. But the price is
too high if it means always being on guard,
constantly suspicious of others. Even an over-
dose of trust that at times involves the risk of
being deceived or disappointed is wiser, in the
long run, than taking it for granted that most
people are incompetent or insincere.

5. The ability to do without constant approval and recognition from others. Particularly in a work situation, the need for constant approval can be harmful and counterproductive. It should not really matter how many people *like* leaders. The important thing is the quality of work that results from collaborating with them. The emotionally wise leader realizes that this quality will suffer when undue emphasis is placed on being a "good guy." More important, it is a large part of the leader's job to take risks. And risks by their very nature cannot be pleasing to everyone.

Positive self-regard may not be found everywhere or in as many places as we'd like to see it. And it's not all that clear how it's acquired—although we'll have more to say about that in our final chapter. One thing that has become clear to us is that to understand and possess positive self-regard does not blind one to the less desirable qualities of human beings; it does, however, establish standards for thinking about human possibilities. It's a way of developing, per-haps, an *atmosphere* of excellence, of greatness.

The Deployment of Self Through the Wallenda Factor

Being on the tightrope is living;
everything else is waiting.

Karl Wallenda, 1968

Most people don't really believe in success. They feel helpless before they even begin. "Whitey's" not keeping the blacks down. He's not keeping us from jobs or education. We have the power to make it in this society and so we can't blame the system for everything. It's the fear of failure that gets in the way.

John H. Johnson
Publisher of *Ebony*

Perhaps the most impressive and memorable quality of the leaders we studied was the way they responded to failure. Like Karl Wallenda, the great tightrope aerialist—whose life was at stake each time he walked the tightrope—these leaders put all their energies into their task. They simply don't think about failure, don't even use the word, relying on such synonyms as "mistake," "glitch," "bungle," or countless others such as "false start," "mess," "hash," "bollix," "setback," and "error." Never *failure*. One of them said during the course of an interview that "a mistake is just another way of doing things." Another said, "If I have an art form of leadership, it is to make as many mistakes as quickly as I can in order to learn." One recalled Harry Truman's famous maxim, "Whenever I make a bum decision, I just go out and make another one."

Shortly after Wallenda fell to his death in 1978 (traversing a 75-foot high wire in downtown San Juan, Puerto Rico), his wife, also an aerialist, discussed that fateful San Juan walk, "perhaps his most dangerous." She recalled: "All Karl thought about for three straight months prior to it was *falling*. It was the first time he'd ever thought about that, and it seemed to me that he put all his energies into *not falling* rather than walking the tightrope." Mrs. Wallenda added that her husband even went so far as to personally supervise the installation of the tightrope, making certain that the guy wires were secure, "something he had never even thought of doing before."

From what we learned from the interviews with successful leaders, it became increasingly clear that when Karl Wallenda poured his energies into *not falling* rather than walking the tightrope, he was virtually destined to fail.

An example of the Wallenda factor came in an interview with Fletcher Byrom, former president of the Koppers Company, a diversified engineering, construction and chemicals company. When asked about the "hardest decision he ever had to make," he responded this way:

> I don't know what a hard decision is. I may be a strange animal but I don't worry. Whenever I make a decision, I start out recognizing there's a strong likelihood I'm going to be wrong. All I can do is the best I can. To worry puts obstacles in the way of clear thinking.

Or consider Ray Meyer—perhaps the winningest coach in college basketball, who led DePaul University to forty-two consecutive years of winning seasons. When his team dropped its first game after twenty-nine straight home court victories, we called to see how he felt about it. His response was vintage Wallenda: "Great! Now we can start concentrating on winning, *not* on not losing." Meyer reframed for us what we're now referring to as the Wallenda factor, the capacity to embrace positive goals, to pour one's energies into the task, not into looking behind and dredging up excuses for past events.

For a lot of people, the word "failure" carries with it a finality, the absence of movement characteristic of a dead thing, to which the automatic human reaction is helpless discouragement. But for the successful leader, failure is a beginning, the springboard to hope.

Examples abound from our research. Former mayor Tom Bradley of Los Angeles, upon being asked about being defeated in his gubernatorial race, said:

> Yes, of course, I was disappointed with the outcome of the election in view of the close margin by which I lost. But it was not the first experience for me in losing a contest. I always come back. I always hang in there. I don't see any reason to change now. I certainly have no intention of retiring from the field of politics. I will keep my options open. And an option for me would be running for governor again.

And then there is Harold Prince, the Broadway producer. He regularly called a press conference the morning after one of his Broadway plays opened—before reading the reviews—in order to announce plans for his *next* play.

Perhaps our best example of the Wallenda factor is that of William Smithburg, the chairman of Quaker

Oats. After two key "mistakes" that Smithburg took responsibility for—the acquisition of a small video game business (since closed) and the French pet accessory business he bought and then wrote off—he said at a meeting with sixty of his food product marketeers, "There isn't one senior manager in this company who hasn't been associated with a product that flopped. That includes me. It's like learning to ski. If you're not falling down, you're not learning."

The tension here, integrated by these leaders, is that of *failure* versus *learning*. While we can't say that they exactly hailed failure, they certainly seemed to profit from it. They used the energy springing from paradox to reach higher goals. Almost every "false step" was regarded as an opportunity and not as the end of the world. They were convinced that they could learn—and, more important, that their organizations could learn—how to succeed at whatever they undertook as their vision.

Often the lesson of a positive attitude is learned through experience, as in the case of Harold Williams. When asked about the most formative experience that had shaped him as a leader, he told a story of having been passed over when Norton Simon, Inc., chose a new president:

> And I was very angry about it and really disappointed at the obvious stupidity of the people who were involved in making the choice, and really licking my wounds and feeling sorry for myself. . . . I happened to have an old friend whom I was talking to about it one day, not long

after, and he asked me what was new and I told him and he looked at me and he said, "Did you ever stop to think why they might be right?" And I couldn't say I had, but at that point, I did. And when I could look and I could start listening—maybe there were reasons why they could have been right. The most important learning experience I had (while I still would have obviously made the other decision), but by golly . . . I sure could understand it . . . and from that . . . I learned a few things. Next time around, they didn't pass me over.

Criticism is a frequent by-product of significant actions. Receptivity to criticism is as necessary as it is loathsome. It tests the foundations of positive self-regard as does nothing else. And the more valid the criticism, the more difficult it is to receive.

Werner Erhard's popular est seminars received so much attention, it was inevitable that some of it would be vituperative and sometimes unfounded. Here he talks about response to criticism:

It is very clear to me that one fails in one's own integrity when one stops to meet an attack—when the "attack" of it has such an effect that you stop the meeting. I know lots of people who have really been buckled by criticism. Their [subsequent] conversation is shot through with answers to criticism which no one in the current environment is expressing. So that's the first thing: *do not stop to meet the attack.*

However, that leaves one open to ignoring the attack which, in my view, is equally detrimental since it leads to lack of integrity. The attack must somehow be included ... accepted—but by accepted I do not mean "agreed with." By accepted I mean "allowed" to be there if one is to be on this path.

Then the question becomes, "How can I use it? How does this attack move me along on this path?" And lots of attacks have kept us from making mistakes we otherwise would have made. For example. Having been attacked for something we weren't doing, we knew not to do it! Or, we could look to see if it was an appropriate thing to do, and we could even see some propensity to move in that direction so the attack would have some genuine validity.

Now about the attacks that are accurate.... They are the most difficult to deal with ... difficult to say, "Yes, that's right. I'm a jerk. I've made a mistake." Because always, or at least for the most part, in my case I'm always in the process of correcting my mistakes. As a matter of fact, even when I am handling it (accepting criticism), I'm sometimes handling it as a way of avoiding confronting it! So *the valid attacks are very useful in that they are an opportunity to complete one's relationship with one's own failing.*

The Wallenda factor is basically about learning, which is a generalization of the word "trying." And all learning involves some "failure," something from which one can continue to learn. Indeed, we can propose a general rule for all organizations: "Reasonable failure should never be received with anger." Spinoza announced a principle very much like this. He said that the highest activity a human being can attain is learning, or, in his language, understanding. To understand is to be free. He argued that those who respond to failure of others by anger are themselves slaves to passion and learn nothing.

Tom Watson, Sr., IBM's founder and its guiding inspiration for over forty years, put that Spinozan principle to work a number of years ago, probably without knowing the source of his action. A promising junior executive of IBM was involved in a risky venture for the company and managed to lose over $10 million in the gamble. It was a disaster. When Watson called the nervous executive into his office, the young man blurted out, "I guess you want my resignation?" Watson said, "You can't be serious. We've just spent $10 million educating you!"

Although leading is a "job" for which leaders are handsomely paid, where their rewards come from—and what they truly value—is a sense of adventure and play. In our interviews, they describe work in ways that scientists use: "exploring a new space," "solving a problem," "designing or discovering something new." Like explorers, scientists, and artists, they seem to focus their attention on a limited field—their task—to forget personal problems, to lose their sense of time, to feel competent and in control. When these elements are present, leaders truly enjoy what they're doing and stop worrying about whether the activity will be productive or not, whether their activities will be rewarded or not, whether what they are doing will work or not. They are walking the tightrope.

We're now at the point where we can bring together the two elements of the management of self into a unified theory. Both positive self-regard and the Wallenda factor have to do basically with the outcomes. In the case of self-regard, the basic question is: how competent *am I*? Do I have "the right stuff"? The Wallenda factor is primarily concerned with one's perception of the *outcome of the event*. If we conceive of these two factors in a negative way, our theory can be clarified. People can give up trying because they seriously doubt that they can do what's required. That's negative self-regard. Or they may be assured of their competencies but give up trying because they expect their efforts to produce no results whatsoever. It's as if Karl Wallenda decided not to walk the tightrope because of wind conditions or the faultiness of the high wire.

Another example might help. Drivers who judge themselves incompetent in navigating winding mountain roads will conjure up outcomes of wreckage and bodily injury, whereas those who are fully confident of their driving capabilities will anticipate sweeping vistas rather than tangled wreckage. For the most part the social reactions people anticipate depend on their judgments on how adroitly they can perform. That's another way for thinking about positive (or negative) self-regard.

The Wallenda factor has less to do with one's judg-

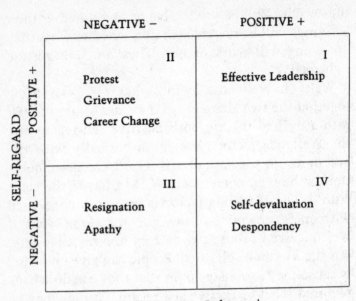

Fig. 2. Wallenda Factor (Outcome Judgment).

ment about self-efficacy than it does about the judgment of the *outcome* of the event. In organizational settings, the expectation of success (take a major capital investment or an important acquisition as examples) can often be dissociated from one's judgment of personal competence. In short, self-regard has to do with a judgment about one's competence, whereas the Wallenda factor has to do with extrinsic outcomes. Expected outcomes are often partially separable from self-regard judgments when extrinsic outcomes are fixed, for example, to a minimal level of performance, as when a designated level of work pro-

ductivity produces a fixed pay but higher performance brings no additional monetary benefits.*

For successful leadership to occur there has to be a
fusion between positive self-regard and optimism
about a desired outcome. And this was clearly the
case for our effective leaders. What seemed to be present in our ninety leaders is one other thing we've
wondered about from time to time, a felicitous
fusion between work and play. Similar to a line from
a Robert Frost poem, "where love and need are one."
We've concluded that great leaders are like the Zen
archer who develops his skills to the point where the
desire to hit the target becomes extinguished and
man, arrow and target become indivisible components of the same process. That's good for leaders.
And when this style of influence works to attract and
empower people to join them on the tightrope, that's
good for organizations and for society.

EMPOWERMENT: THE DEPENDENT VARIABLE

To lead,
   One must follow.

Lao-tzu

Now we come to the quintessential question: What's
the effect of this style of leadership on the work
force? We've hinted at this in our preceding para-
graph, so it should come as no surprise that leaders

*We are indebted to the work of Albert Bandura for this analysis.[5]

both create and catch. Put another way, they *empower others to translate intention into reality and sustain it.* This does not mean that leaders must relinquish power, or that followers must continually challenge authority. It does mean that power must become a unit of exchange—an active, changing token in creative, productive and communicative transactions. Effective leaders will ultimately reap the human harvest of their efforts by the simple action of power's reciprocal: *empowerment.* It puts the duality in *motion*—power to empowerment, empowerment back to power. Almost the way conductor and players or leaders and subordinates play off one another, building into a crescendo of harmonious voices, an epiphany of human effort. This reciprocity creates its own rhythm, its own vitality and momentum.

The essential thing in organizational leadership is that the leader's style *pulls* rather than *pushes* people on. A pull style of influence works by attracting and energizing people to an exciting vision of the future. It motivates by identification, rather than through rewards and punishments. The leaders we have been talking about articulate and embody the ideals toward which the organization is striving. They enroll themselves (and others) in a vision of that ideal as attainable and worthy.

Leading is a responsibility, and the effectiveness of this responsibility is reflected in the attitudes of the led. We've come to discover that these attitudes consist of four critical dimensions of the workforce, what we refer to as empowerment.

Before getting to the dimensions of empowerment,

it may be useful to learn about the unusual route we took to get to our understanding of the concept. It was after our final interview with Harold Williams. He had recently left the chairmanship of the SEC and was in his new office atop a skyscraper in Century City, Los Angeles. He had been reflecting on his experiences in Washington and proudly displayed a book of his speeches, which his staff had bound in beautiful buckram leather on the occasion of his departure from the SEC. The inscriptions in the inside cover were revealing:

It was all great fun! Ralph

Working with you was one of my finest professional experiences. They will long endure long after your work at the Commission is over. Amy

You saw and understood us in a singular way and in the process you gave meaning and significance to our professional lives. Mark

Sometimes it came easy; often it did not. Always it was a learning and maturing experience. You taught us about thoughtful judgment and the need to have a sense of the times—how to cultivate it and how to convey it. Always it was fun! Thanks! George

The opportunity to work with you was a fine form of postgraduate education for me. I hope it was as enjoyable and stimulating for you as it was for me. Dan

If we review carefully what Williams's staff inscribed on the inside cover of their tribute, the mystery of empowerment unravels somewhat. For Mark it is *significance*. Almost exactly like the other staff members we became acquainted with, he felt that he was making a difference both for the organization and in the greater context of the world. We discovered that the effective leader seemed able to create a vision that gave workers the feeling of being at the active centers of the social order. Such "centers" have nothing to do with geometry and nothing to do with pop management bromides. What they do do is get the organization (and its workforce) to concentrate on serious acts. These serious acts consist of areas in society where its leading ideas and institutions come together to create an arena in which the events that most vitally affect people's lives take place. It is an involvement with such arenas and with the momentous events that occur in them that "translates intentions into reality." It is not popular appeal or inventive craziness we have in mind but being near the heart of things, whether it is "getting Frito-Lay chips to the little grocer in Leadville, Colorado," as Wayne Calloway, CEO of Frito-Lay, put it, or Neil Armstrong's participation in the first moon shot.

The second component of empowerment is *competence*, meaning development and learning on the job. As Dan (above) said—and as we heard repeatedly—work was a "fine form of postgraduate education." This increasing sense of mastery and ever-new horizons enhanced performance and alignment behind the organization's goals.

Thirdly, workers experienced something akin to "family," to *community*. They felt joined in some common purpose. Although this doesn't come through sharply in the homages to Williams, it was there, in the way the workers perceived the organization, nonetheless. We're not talking necessarily about a matter of "liking" one another. Rather, it is a sense of reliance on one another toward a common cause that we have in mind. This component includes what one executive at Intel referred to as "that occasional epiphany which occurs when an exquisitely complicated effort is coordinated and completed well."

The fourth aspect of empowerment, *enjoyment* or just plain *fun*, comes through in almost all of the encomiums to Williams and in statements by countless other members of the organizations where we interviewed. This should put to rest all those speculations that one must lead through ever-imminent punishment or simply with the carrot and stick. Old theories of motivation qualified innate and learned responses toward satisfying basic needs. They suggested that one can derive enjoyment only from a finite number of experiences and objects. Therefore, life must be inherently painful because scarce pleasure resources lead to competition, and only the very few will get more than intermittent satisfaction. All theories of behavior that reduce enjoyment or fun to the satisfaction of needs, whether they are held by economists or behaviorists, come to the same conclusion—that needs can never be fully satisfied. We need not elaborate on the destructive and even desperate situations this paradigm has produced.

Through empowerment, however, workers seem to get so immersed in their game of work that they forget basic needs for long periods of time. We see people involved in diverse job-related activities that provide none of the rewards which "need reduction" theorists deem inevitable. If this is true, as we believe, almost any object or experience can be made fun or is at least potentially enjoyable. That enjoyment does not depend on scarce resources. Thus, empowerment ameliorates not only the quality of work life but life itself.

PLAN FOR IMPLEMENTATION

The next four chapters are organized around each of the four major themes just set forth, which encompass our theory of transformative leadership and empowerment. Starting now, our emphasis will shift from the leader as an individual with certain personal attributes to the leader of an organization. Putting it more precisely, our focus will change from leader effectiveness to organizational effectiveness. Accordingly, the next four chapters will address the implementation of our theory or how, more simply, leaders empower organizations.

Thus, for example, the next chapter will concentrate on how an organization *creates* an appropriate and *compelling vision* of the future, while the chapter on Strategy II will show how the *management of meaning* translates into the requisite social architecture that can enable the organization actually to realize its vision. The next chapter takes up the question of how to *position the organization* correctly in the outside world and how the leader designs and controls relationships with major constituencies in a complex, ambiguous, and uncertain environment. The chapter on Strategy IV addresses the issue of *organizational learning,* the organizational correlate of the *management of self.*

Note that each of the following four chapters, to a greater or lesser extent, relates to and builds on each of the themes addressed in this chapter. *Vision,* for example, will be the focus of inquiry for the chapter on Strategy I. In the chapter on Strategy II we will address the *management of meaning* from which the social architecture will spring, which, in turn, will enable the organization to bring its vision into being.

The fit between leader effectiveness and organizational effectiveness isn't always perfect, of course, but analogies abound, and we believe that it is important to keep this split vision in constant view.

The important thing to keep in mind in the remainder of the book is that nothing serves an organization better—especially during times of agonizing doubts and uncertainties—than leadership that knows what it wants, communicates those intentions, positions itself correctly, and empowers its workforce. But though these laws sound simple, their implementation requires certain skills. These techniques are the subject of the following chapters.

STRATEGY I: ATTENTION THROUGH VISION

> Both Mr. Durant and Mr. Ford had unusual vision,
> courage, daring, imagination, and foresight. Both
> gambled everything on the future of the automobile
> at a time when fewer were made in a year than are
> now made in a couple of days. . . . Both created great
> and lasting institutions.
>
> Alfred P. Sloan, Jr.

> I have a dream.
>
> Martin Luther King, Jr.

When William Paley took over at CBS in 1928 at the
age of 27, the network had no stations of its own, was
losing money, and was insignificant in an industry
completely dominated by NBC. Within ten years, CBS

had 114 stations and was earning $27.7 million. More than forty years later, with Paley still at the helm, CBS was a dominant force in the broadcasting industry. As David Halberstam has described Paley's ability:

> The critical years were the early ones. What he had from the start was a sense of vision, a sense of what might be. It was as if he could sit in New York in his tiny office with his almost bankrupt company and see not just his own desk, or the row of potential advertisers outside along Madison Avenue, but millions of the American people out in the hinterlands, so many of them out there, almost alone, many of them in homes as yet unconnected to electricity, people alone with almost no form of entertainment other than radio. It was his sense, his confidence that he could reach them, that he had something for them, that made him different. He could envision the audience at a time when there was in fact no audience. He not only had the vision, he knew how to harness it, he could see that the larger the audience, the greater the benefit to the network, because it would mean that many more advertisers would want to participate. . . . The larger the audience, the more time he could sell. To achieve that goal, he had something to offer—indeed to give away—by making his programs available to affiliate stations.[1]

Over and over again, the leaders we spoke to told us that they did the same things when they took charge of their organizations—they paid attention to what was going on, they determined what part of the events at hand would be important for the future of the organization, they set a new direction, and they concentrated the attention of everyone in the organization on it. We soon found that this was a universal principle of leadership, as true for orchestra conductors, army generals, football coaches, and school superintendents as for corporate leaders. But if it all seems too easy, there is a catch. How do leaders know what is important for the future of their organizations, and how do they choose the new directions? That is what we must examine; but first we need to discuss why we think the principle works and why it is so fundamental to effective leadership.

VISION AND ORGANIZATIONS

To choose a direction, a leader must first have developed a mental image of a possible and desirable future state of the organization. This image, which we call a *vision*, may be as vague as a dream or as precise as a goal or mission statement. The critical point is that a vision articulates a view of a realistic, credible, attractive future for the organization, a condition that is better in some important ways than what now exists.

A vision is a target that beckons. When John Kennedy set a goal of putting a man on the moon by 1970 or Bill Gates aimed to put a computer on every desk and in every home, they were focusing attention on worthwhile and attainable achievements. Note also that a vision always refers to a *future* state, a condition that does not presently exist and never existed before. With a vision, the leader provides the all-important bridge from the present to the future of the organization.

To understand why vision is so central to leadership success, we only need reflect on why organizations are formed in the first place. An organization is a group of people engaged in a common enterprise. Individuals join the enterprise in the hope of receiving rewards for their participation. Depending upon the organization and the individuals involved, the rewards might be largely economic, or they might be dominated by psychosocial considerations—status, self-esteem, a sense of accomplishment, a meaningful existence. Just as the individual derives rewards from his or her role in the organization, so too does the organization derive its rewards from finding an appropriate niche in the larger society. The organization's rewards might also be economic (profits, growth, access to resources) or psychosocial (prestige, legitimacy, power and recognition).

So, on the one hand, an organization seeks to maximize its rewards from its position in the external environment and, on the other hand, individuals in the organization seek to maximize their reward from their participation in the organization. When the organization has a clear sense of its purpose, direction, and desired future state and when this image is widely shared, individuals are able to find their own roles both in the organization and in the larger society of which they are a part. This empowers individuals and confers status upon them because they can see themselves as part of a worthwhile enterprise. They gain a sense of importance, as they are transformed from robots blindly following instructions to human beings engaged in a creative and purposeful venture. When individuals feel that they can make a difference and that they can improve the society in which they are living through their participation in an organization, then it is much more likely that they will bring vigor and enthusiasm to their tasks and that the results of their work will be mutually reinforcing. Under these conditions, the human energies of the organization are aligned toward a common end, and a major precondition for success has been satisfied.

Consultants often report that they can feel this energy almost from the first moment they enter a corporation. It was present at Polaroid when Edwin Land led that firm into a new age of photography, and at Starbucks when Howard Schultz transformed a few coffee shops in Seattle into national leadership in the specialty-coffee industry. It takes the form of enthusiasm, commitment, pride, willingness to work hard and "go the extra mile." It is notably absent in some of the large conglomerates, where every month brings a new deal that proclaims to the employees that management is going into or out of a new business—or, more likely, isn't really sure where it is going.

A shared vision of the future also suggests measures of effectiveness for the organization and for all its parts. It helps individuals distinguish between what's good and what's bad for the organization, and what it's worthwhile to want to achieve. And most important, it makes it possible to distribute decision making widely. People can make difficult decisions without having to appeal to higher levels in the organization each time because they know what end results are desired. Thus, in a very real sense, individual behavior can be shaped, directed, and coordinated by a shared and empowering vision of the future.

As John Young, former head of Hewlett-Packard, said, "Successful companies have a consensus from top to bottom on a set of overall goals. The most brilliant management strategy will fail if that consensus is missing."[2]

We have here one of the clearest distinctions between the leader and the manager. By focusing attention on a vision, the leader operates on the *emotional and spiritual resources* of the organization, on its values, commitment and aspirations. The manager, by contrast, operates on the *physical resources* of the organization, on its capital, human skills, raw materials and technology. Any competent manager can make it possible for people in the organization to earn a living. An excellent manager can see to it that work is done productively and efficiently, on schedule, and with a high level of quality. It remains for the effective leader, however, to help people in the organization know pride and satisfaction in their work. Great leaders often inspire their followers to high levels of achievement by showing them how their work contributes to worthwhile ends. It is an emotional appeal to some of the most fundamental of human needs—the need to be important, to make a difference, to feel useful, to be a part of a successful and worthwhile enterprise.

With all of these benefits, one would think that organizations would take great care to develop a clear image of their desired future, but that doesn't seem to be the case. Instead, the visions of many organizations are out of focus and lack coherence. The reasons for this blurred focus are myriad.

- Within the past several decades, important new interpretations have been given to the role of the family, the quality of life, the work ethic, the social responsibility of business, the rights of minorities, and many other values and institutions that were once thought to be enduring and permanent.
- Telecommunications and rapid transportation have helped make the world increasingly interdependent for products, ideas, jobs, and resources.
- The quickening pace of innovation has led to the specialization of experts and massive problems of coordinating technical workers.
- The general willingness to experiment with new social forms and norms has fractured society into a diversity of lifestyles, each with its own product preferences.
- Workers are seeking and receiving a much greater voice in decisions that were once the exclusive territory of management.

All these forces and more contribute to the massive and growing complexity we see in today's world. This, in turn, creates great uncertainty and an overabundance of conflicting images in many organizations. The larger the organization, the greater the number of images is likely to be, the greater their complexity of interaction, and the quicker their shift in emphasis over time.

All these things tend to cause organizational vertigo and lead to myopia. At the same time, they tend to make vision more imperative for the functional success of the organization, since without a coherent view of the future, these forces would conspire to shatter it in every direction. This explains, for example, why George Fisher had to be hired away from Motorola to provide a new focus and sense of purpose to the giant, century-old Eastman-Kodak Company. Weakened by years of competitive inroads into its strong traditional markets—cameras, film and film developing—and unable to stake out major positions in newer markets like plain-paper copiers, Eastman-Kodak had become nearly paralyzed by conflicting images of where it should be headed. A bold new vision was needed to reorient the firm toward a twenty-first–century technology—digital photography—with all that entails: selling off nonimaging businesses, developing digital cameras and forming strategic alliances with other high tech firms like Microsoft and IBM. But where does the leader's vision come from?

PAYING ATTENTION:
THE LEADER'S SEARCH FOR VISION

Historians tend to write about great leaders as if they possessed transcendent genius, as if they were capable of creating their visions and sense of destiny out of some mysterious inner resource. Perhaps some do, but upon closer examination it usually turns out that the vision did not originate with the leader personally but rather from others. For example, Harold Williams told us that when he arrived at UCLA to take his new position as dean of its Graduate School of Management, "It was really the faculty that brought together the concept of what it is we ought to do. They had the vision." Other leaders looked elsewhere. John Kennedy spent a great deal of time reading history and studying the ideas of great thinkers. Martin Luther King, Jr., found many of his ideas in the study of religious and ethical ideologies as well as in the traditions of his own and other peoples. Lenin was greatly influenced by the scholarship of Karl Marx, in much the same way as many contemporary business leaders are influenced by the works of leading economists and management scholars. Alfred P. Sloan's visions for the future of General Motors were greatly shaped by the prevailing cultural paradigm— the "American Dream" and the role of capitalism in it. Bill Gates at Microsoft and Andrew Grove at Intel were able to develop their visions from logical processes, mostly by seeking the technical limits of known technologies.

In all these cases, the leader may have been the one

who chose the image from those available at the moment, articulated it, gave it form and legitimacy, and focused attention on it, but the leader only rarely was the one who conceived of the vision in the first place. Therefore, the leader must be a superb listener, particularly to those advocating new or different images of the emerging reality. Many leaders establish both formal and informal channels of communication to gain access to these ideas. Most leaders also spend a substantial portion of their time interacting with advisers, consultants, other leaders, scholars, planners, and a wide variety of other people both inside and outside their own organizations in this search. Successful leaders, we have found, are *great askers*, and they do pay attention.

Consider a typical example. Suppose you've been asked to take charge of a regional bank operating in the state of California. The board of directors has turned to you for leadership as a result of your success with a smaller bank in another state. How will you develop a sense of direction in your new circumstances? To whom will you pay attention, and how, to help you develop an appropriate vision of the future? Basically, there are three sources from which to seek guidance—the past, the present and alternative images of future possibilities. We'll consider each of these in turn.

The Past

One obvious way to start is to reflect on your own experiences with other banks to identify analogies and precedents that might apply to the new situation. Next, you'll talk to leaders at other banks to collect their experiences with different approaches. You will surely want to learn about the history of the bank you are joining so you'll be able to understand how it reached its current status and what qualities contributed to its past successes and failures. This you'll get by talking to a wide variety of your new colleagues up and down the organization.

As you do this, you'll be building a mental model of what worked and what didn't work for this and similar banks in the past. You will be identifying some long-term trends—say, in deposits or loan experiences—that might be projected into the future as a first approximation of where the bank is heading if it continues as in the past. You'll collect thoughts about how the bank's performance has been linked to outside indicators—say, the state of the economy, interest rates or development of the local community. And, of course, you'll pay attention to all the historical data you can get your hands on to increase your understanding of what this particular bank has been trying to do in the past, how successful it has been and why.

The Present

There is a lot to learn about the future from looking all around you at what is happening right now. For example, if you think about the year 2020, most of the buildings, roads, cities, people, corporations and government agencies that will exist then are already here. The present provides a first approximation of the human, organizational and material resources out of which the future will be formed. By studying these resources, it is possible to develop an understanding of the constraints and opportunities for their use and the conditions under which they may grow, decline, interact or self-destruct. As a banker, you'll pay a lot of attention to your current managers and their potential for development, to your current customer mix and the opportunities for expanding the services offered to them, to the locations of your branches, to your existing loan portfolios and to what your competitors are doing.

There are early warning signals of impending change all around you. Your market researchers, for example, should be able to identify growing markets at an early stage of development. The plans of politicians and business leaders are often widely reported. Public opinion polls document changing values and needs, and special surveys in your own field of financial services are often reported in the trade press. In fact, trend monitoring to provide early warning is a large and growing industry in the United States.

Finally, you can conduct small experiments in your own bank. Suppose you are considering a major refocusing of the bank's attention in the direction of, say, loans for small businesses, or the professions, or particular industries. You can set up one branch or a small division with instructions to devote all its energies to the chosen area for some period of time, just as a chemical company develops a pilot plant before making a major commitment. You have, in effect, created a laboratory in which to experiment with your new vision.

The Future

Your vision for the bank, as we have pointed out, will have to be set in some future time, so you need to study the conditions that may prevail at that time. Actually, although no one can predict what these conditions will be, there are many clues. Some sources of information have already been discussed— long-term trends, particularly in demography and resource usage; planning documents at the international, national, state and corporate levels; the intentions and visions of policymakers in all kinds of organizations; public opinion polls; and the leading edges of phenomena that are expected to increase greatly in the future. But there are a few more sources of information.

You could look for structural clues to the future. For example, you might conclude that unless the government reverses its recent deregulation decisions, strong new competitors will continue to enter the banking business and a major restructuring of the industry will occur. You could then look at the kinds of structural changes and commitments being made by some of these potential competitors—Charles Schwab, American Express, Japanese and other foreign banks and so on—and develop a scenario of what the marketplace may look like if all these changes are made. You could then go on to examine the implications of such a scenario for specific customer groups, for the economy in general, for the investment community and ultimately for the banking industry and your particular bank.

Beyond structural clues, you could obtain forecasts of all kinds to study: economic projections, demographic analyses, industry forecasts and the like. You could explore some of the intellectual ideas that may shape the future: philosophical works; science fiction novels; political party platforms; and books by leading sociologists, political scientists and futurists. There are harbingers of future technological developments in research and development laboratories, technical papers presented at professional meetings and government reports.

Thus, far from being devoid of information, you are likely to be inundated with information about the future, though only a small part may provide useful benchmarks or signposts in developing your vision for the bank. It is in the *interpretation* of this information that the real art of leadership lies. Just as the historian attempts to take piles of information about the past and construct an interpretation of the forces that may have been at work, so does the leader select, organize, structure and interpret information about the future in an attempt to construct a viable and credible vision. But the leader has one distinctive advantage over the historian in that much of the future can be invented or designed. By synthesizing an appropriate vision, the leader is influential in shaping the future itself.

SYNTHESIZING VISION:
THE LEADER'S CHOICE OF DIRECTION

All of the leaders to whom we spoke seemed to have been masters at selecting, synthesizing and articulating an appropriate vision of the future. Later, we learned that this was a common quality of leaders down through the ages. Consider, for example, how a contemporary biographer of Napoleon, Louis Madelin, described him:

> He would deal with three or four alternatives at the same time and endeavor to conjure up every possible eventuality—preferably the worst. This foresight, the fruit of meditation, generally enabled him to be ready for any setback; nothing ever took him by surprise. . . . His vision, as I have said, was capable of both breadth and depth. Perhaps the most astonishing characteristic of his intellect was the combination of idealism and realism which enabled him to face the most exalted visions at the same time as the most insignificant realities. And, indeed, he was in a sense a visionary, a dreamer of dreams.[3]

The task of synthesizing an appropriate direction for the organization is complicated by the many dimensions of vision that may be required. Leaders require *foresight*, so that they can judge how the vision fits into the way the environment of the organization may evolve; *hindsight*, so that the vision does not violate the traditions and culture of the organization;

a worldview, within which to interpret the impact of possible new developments and trends; *depth perception*, so that the whole picture can be seen in appropriate detail and perspective; *peripheral vision*, so that the possible responses of competitors and other stakeholders to the new direction can be comprehended; and a process of *revision*, so that all visions previously synthesized are constantly reviewed as the environment changes. Beyond this, decisions must be made about the appropriate time horizon to address, the simplicity or complexity of the image, the extent to which it will represent continuity with the past as opposed to a radical transformation, the degree of optimism or pessimism it will contain, its realism and credibility, and its potential impact on the organization.

If there is a spark of genius in the leadership function at all, it must lie in this transcending ability, a kind of magic, to assemble—out of all the variety of images, signals, forecasts and alternatives—a clearly articulated vision of the future that is at once simple, easily understood, clearly desirable, and energizing.

Let's return to our banker example to see what might be involved. To this point, we have suggested how, as a new leader, you might collect all kinds of information that provides the raw material for a new vision of the future. Since vision cannot be limitless and still be credible to people in the organization, you will need to draw some boundaries. The vision should be projected in time and space beyond the boundaries of ordinary planning activities in the bank, but it should not be so far distant as to be beyond the ability of incumbents in the organization to realize. Perhaps you will decide to focus on a ten-year goal, far enough away to permit really dramatic change and yet within the comprehension and career aspirations of much of the current workforce. Perhaps too, you will want to move beyond the boundaries of current operations to include major new fields of activity such as personal financial planning or international banking or to focus on a broad range of services to one or more specific target markets, such as high-technology industry.

The actual boundaries chosen will depend heavily on values as well. Your own values will determine which alternatives you seriously consider and the way they are evaluated. For example, Harold Williams now heads the J. Paul Getty Museum and Foundation, but his values were formed during a distinguished career in industry, academia, and public service. Thus, it is not surprising that he is steering the Getty Foundation in the direction of preservation and scholarship and has promised not to allow the vast Getty fortune to be used to bid art prices up so high that other museums will be unable to acquire new works or serve their publics.

The values of the rest of the people in the bank, as reflected in the prevailing ideology, also suggest limits to the amount of change that might reasonably be expected. Values, for example, might dictate that whatever the new vision for the future of the bank is, it should emphasize quality and excellence of service rather than price or breadth of service.

With information and some boundary conditions

in mind, you will try to understand the possible alternatives and weigh how attractive they are. Your most powerful tool for this purpose is the mental model you have built up over time of how the world works and how your bank operates in it. As a wise leader, you will have tested this mental model many times in discussions with key executives, consultants, and others who have also thought deeply about the future of the bank. If you have access to a computer modeling facility and if the occasion justifies the cost, then a more formal, quantitative model can also be built.

Much of this analysis will have to be a series of "judgment calls," but it is possible to suggest some of the questions that should be addressed, including the following:

- What are the institutions that have a stake in the future of this bank, and what is it that they would like to see happen?
- What are the possible indicators of performance for the bank, and how can they be measured?
- What would happen to the bank if it continued on its present path without any major changes?
- What early warning signals might you detect if the external environment of the bank were in fact to change substantially?
- What could you do to alter the course of events, and what would the consequences of your actions be?
- What resources does your bank possess or can

it obtain to act in the various futures that are possible?

- Of the alternative possible futures for the bank and its environments, which are more likely to be favorable to survival and success?

Through a series of questions such as these, patterns may appear that suggest viable alternative visions. You must then synthesize all this information into a single vision, and here is where the art form of leadership really comes into play. The synthesis of a vision involves a great degree of judgment and, not infrequently, considerable intuition and creativity as well.

In a book called *Visionary Leadership* and in two other recent books,[4] one of the authors showed how a leader can conduct a retreat with a small group of colleagues to develop a new vision over a period of a few days. Involving others in the visioning process allows the participants to share their values and dreams, brings a broader range of viewpoints and expertise into the search for a new direction, and makes it easier to gain commitment to the vision at the end of the process. A vision retreat is a group process that systematically explores new vision possibilities in four phases:

1. Vision Audit, which examines the character of the organization, including its current mission, strategy and values.
2. Vision Scope, in which decisions are made regarding the desired characteristics of the new vision.

3. Vision Context, which explores trends and developments that influence the formation of a new vision.
4. Vision Choice, in which alternative visions are identified and evaluated, leading to a final selection of the most desirable option.

Let us assume that in the banking example, you have decided that the future of your bank, all things considered, would be most enhanced if it concentrated its attention on serving high-technology companies, particularly in newly emerging industries, with a wide range of financial services. It still remains to translate this vision into action.

FOCUSING ATTENTION: THE LEADER'S SEARCH FOR COMMITMENT

The leader may generate new views of the future and may be a genius at synthesizing and articulating them, but this makes a difference only when the vision has been successfully communicated throughout the organization and effectively institutionalized as a guiding principle. Leaders are only as powerful as the ideas they can communicate. The leader's basic philosophy must be: "We have seen what this organization can be, we understand the consequences of that vision, and now we must act to make it so."

A vision cannot be established in an organization by edict, or by the exercise of power or coercion. It is more an act of persuasion, of creating an enthusiastic and dedicated commitment to a vision because it is right for the times, right for the organization, and right for the people who are working in it.

We have found in our discussions with leaders that visions can often be communicated best by metaphors, or models—as when a political leader promises "a chicken in every pot" or a phone company encourages you to "reach out and touch someone." Perhaps in our banking example, it might be something like "innovative banking for innovative companies," or "financial services at the leading edge."

In any communication, some distortion takes place, but the great leader seems to be able to find just the right metaphor that clarifies the idea and minimizes distortion. In fact, the right metaphor often transcends verbal communication altogether; like a good poem or song, it is much more than mere words. It "feels right," it appeals at the gut level, it resonates with the listener's own emotional needs, it somehow "clicks."

Another way the leader communicates a new vision is by consistently acting on it and personifying it. Think of the way Martin Luther King, Jr., embodied and communicated the vision of the civil rights movement, or the way Ted Turner showed by his own personal sense of adventure in the America's Cup races the extent of innovation and risk-taking he expected in his company, Turner Broadcasting. Lewis Platt, chairman and CEO of Hewlett Packard, communicates the HP vision in his own less flamboyant way, spending 30 percent of his time with customers and another 30 percent visiting HP's offices in more than 110 countries and, as he says, "tens of hours each week responding to voice mail and E-mail."[5]

A vision of the future is not offered once and for all by the leader and then allowed to fade away. It must be repeated time and time again. It must be incorporated in the organization's culture and reinforced through the strategy and decision-making process. It must be constantly evaluated for possible change in the light of new circumstances.

In the end, the leader may be the one who articulates the vision and gives it legitimacy, who expresses the vision in captivating rhetoric that fires the imagination and emotions of followers, who—through the vision—empowers others to make decisions that get things done. But if the organization is to be successful, the image must grow out of the needs of the entire organization and must be "claimed" or "owned" by all the important actors. In short, it must become part of a new social architecture in the organization, the subject to which we next turn our attention.

STRATEGY II: MEANING THROUGH COMMUNICATION

Above and beyond his envisioning capabilities, a leader must be a *social architect* who understands the organization and shapes the way it works. The social architecture of any organization is the silent variable that translates the "blooming, buzzing confusion" of organizational life into meaning. It determines who says what to whom, about what, and what kinds of actions then ensue. Social architecture is an intangible, but it governs the way people act, the values and norms that are subtly transmitted to groups and individuals, and the construct of binding and bonding within a company.*

Recall that in the chapter called "Leading Others, Managing Yourself" we asked: How do you get people aligned behind the organization's overarching goals? How do you communicate visions? We answered that question partially then by asserting that this can happen through the "management of meaning." But this doesn't go far enough, because it fails to indicate how this actually happens—how the leader creates the understanding, participation and ownership of the vision. In this chapter we will discuss the organizational mechanism through which employees recognize and get behind something of an established identity (the vision). The mechanism is the social architecture, which can facilitate *or* subvert "the best-laid plans."

---

*The meaning of "social architecture" will become clearer as we proceed. For the moment, conceive of it as virtually synonymous with the trendier buzzword "culture," or more simply as the norms and values that shape behavior in any organized setting. We prefer the term "social architecture" for a number of reasons, not the least being its aesthetic edge. But above and beyond our aesthetic preferences, there are stronger reasons for its use here. First of all, it conveys far more meaning than "culture"—the vaguest of terms—does, and it certainly relates *meaning* to organizational life in a way that "organizational culture" doesn't. Perhaps most important, though, is that "social architecture" implies change and tractability and that leaders can do something about it, whereas "culture," as ordinarily used, implies an unbridled rigidity or intractability. Words and phrases are important, and though we tend to use "culture" and "social architecture" interchangeably, we believe that the latter term makes more sense. To the best of our knowledge, the phrase "social architecture" was coined by H. V. Perlmutter.

Despite some conceptual vagueness, which we hope to overcome, social architecture can be defined, assessed and, to a certain extent, shaped and managed. The design and management of social architecture is one of the four pivotal responsibilities of the leader.

A few words about the concept and some reasons for the importance we attach to it. We believe that we human beings are suspended in webs of significance that we ourselves have spun. We view social architecture to be those webs of meaning. In other words, social architecture is that which provides context (or meaning) and commitment to its membership and stakeholders. So, first and foremost, social architecture presents a shared interpretation of organizational events, so that members know how they are expected to behave. It also generates a commitment to the primary organizational values and philosophy—that is, the vision that employees feel they are working for and can believe in. Finally, an organization's social architecture serves as a control mechanism, sanctioning or proscribing particular kinds of behavior.

The significance of social architecture can be readily observed if we examine a specific case where a particular social architecture, once a source of strength, became a major obstacle to future success. The clever reader has probably already guessed that we are referring to AT&T.

The story is well known but bears a quick repetition now: In 1978 AT&T announced that it was making a strategic shift from a service-oriented telephone utility to a market-oriented communications business. Chairman John DeButts went on intra-company TV to announce to every employee that "we will become a marketing company." To implement this new strategy, AT&T undertook the largest organizational transformation in the history of U.S. industry. One out of every three of the million jobs at AT&T were changed. Despite the major changes in structure, in human resources, and in support systems, there was a general consensus both inside and outside AT&T that its greatest task in making its strategy succeed was its ability to transform the AT&T culture. We were intimately involved in working with two of the seven divested "telephone companies," helping to revise the social architecture, and found that it took years before success could be fairly claimed and that even then, there would be lingering effects of the old culture.

How do you get your hands, so to speak, around an organization's social architecture? One man who tried was Walter Spencer, the former president of Sherwin-Williams Company. For six years Spencer attempted to turn around a firm that suffered from an overabundance of unprofitable products that could not, it seemed, be cut, such as an antiquated plant and equipment that could not be written off. There was also the deeply entrenched manufacturing bias held by most board members in the capital-goods-oriented city of Cleveland. Speaking of his attempts to transform Sherwin-Williams from a production-oriented company to a marketing one, Spencer said, "When you take a 100-year-old company and change the culture of the organization and try to do that in Cleveland's traditional business setting . . . well, it takes time. You just have to keep hammering away at everybody." After six years of such "hammering away," Spencer resigned, saying that the job was no longer any fun. He had dented but not changed the culture.[1]

In our experience, the reasons so many experiments in organizational change fail is that the leaders have failed to take into account the strong undertow of cultural forces. Leaders who fail to take their social architecture into account and yet try to change their organizations resemble nothing so much as Canute, the legendary Danish monarch who stood on the beach and commanded the waves to stand still as proof of his power.

Perhaps the following examples can illustrate the significance of this point; the first has to do with the effect of culture in determining the success of mergers and acquisitions and the second with the implementation of corporate strategic plans:

- When marketing-oriented Rockwell International merged with aerospace engineering wizards at North American, managers and analysts alike expected a synergistic reaction. "Rockwell, looking for new technologies and new products for commercial markets, saw North American as a place where 'scientific longhairs' threw away ideas every day that could be useful to Rockwell. North American, in turn, was

attracted to Rockwell's commercial manufacturing muscle."*

- Rather than supporting each other, however, the
basic values of the firms collided. "As then-CEO
Robert Anderson lamented, the aerospace people
weren't used to commercial problems. 'We kept
beating them on the head to diversify, but every
time they'd try it they'd spend a lot of money on
something that, when all is said and done, there
was no market for, or they overdesigned for the
market.'" The world-views of the two firms, as it
turned out, were radically different: "Rockwell's
company culture looked at the world as a rough-
and-tumble place where profit margins dominate
decision-making. North American's environment was more noble. Some sixty well-paid
Ph.D.s, for example, spent only 20 percent of
their time on company business and were free to
devote the rest as they chose to basic research.
*This was not compatible with Rockwell's obses-
sion about controlling costs and margins.*"
Many years later, executives were still trying to
improve the cultural fit of the two firms.[2]

The second example illustrates the impact of corporate culture on innovative programs, specifically a
program designed to improve corporate health:[3]

- American corporations—concerned with
employee health and rising health care costs—

*We are indebted to the work of Howard Schwartz and Stan
Davis throughout this chapter.

are on a health buying spree, installing fitness centers, building gyms, and buying health programs. Thus far this flurry of activity has done little good. Illness rates and illness costs continue to soar, and the evidence shows that few people maintain even the changes in health practices that they are able to make. *The chief reason for the failure of business health programs appears to be that the organizational culture, filled with negative health norms,* *overrides whatever changes the individuals try to make.* Where companies have begun to treat health as a cultural as well as an individual problem, they find hope for long-lasting change in their employees' lives and considerable savings in the company health bill.

All of the above examples point out the significance of social architecture and, we believe, make the case that leaders must learn to deal strategically with it. At this point, it might be useful to summarize how a social architecture comes into being and is maintained.

First, a founder or founding group comes together to produce something or provide a service. The founder(s) have attitudes and values about their prod-

*A number of firms we know of have installed the most expensive state-of-the-art gymnasiums/health centers imaginable. At the same time, these firms induce an unbearable amount of stress through prodigious work loads, unhealthy plant conditions, heavy travel schedules, and anxiety-laden situations, all of which nullify the presumed benefits of their formal "health programs."

uct, and the product or function itself has characteristics that define how it can be performed. In turn, the market, product, or service will be positioned so as to attain a distinctive niche in the environment. (In the next chapter, we discuss at length this process of "positioning.") Then, reward systems will be initiated and evolved to match the attitudes or style of the founding father(s) as well as the goals of the organization and the character of the way processes are performed. As the organization grows, other people join, reinforcing certain aspects of its operation and modifying others—or they leave because they do not fit in or cannot change the operation to their liking.

And the organization continues to evolve and change—in some ways. The tasks, the performance, the market, and the delivery all may shift. The organization becomes larger or smaller, flourishes or stagnates, becomes more homogeneous or more diverse.

At the same time, the social architecture (or culture) does not change commensurately—nor should it necessarily. Sometimes the style of the founding fathers will work in conjunction with change. More often, the style remains but is inappropriate. This style, or organizational culture, which was at first so functional, becomes a separate force, independent and at times at variance with the reasons and incidents that formed it in the first place. In short, when management attempts to shift the goals of the organization, to adopt new work methods, or to create any fundamental change, the culture may not only fail to support these changes but may actually defeat them.

Enough of these abstractions. Let's get down to

cases. What we hope to accomplish in the remainder of this chapter is, first, to identify and describe the three most prominent types of social architecture found in contemporary organizational life. They're archetypes, what Max Weber would call "ideal types." Following that, we'll get down to the most crucial of all questions: How does a leader shape and change the social architecture? So, in the next section, our aim is to deepen the leader's understanding of social architecture and, following that, to equip him with the requisite tools to change it.

THREE STYLES OF SOCIAL ARCHITECTURE

The major elements that define an organization's social architecture are its origins; its basic operating principle; the nature of its work; the management of information, decision making and power; influence; and status. These elements characterize three distinct organizational types—the *collegial, personalistic* and *formalistic*—which we will review below.

A Collegial Organization*

The company was founded on an engineering concept that few people believed in: that a high-technol-

---

*We are more than "deeply indebted" to Marcia Wilkof for this section. Her doctoral dissertation, from which we liberally partook, served as the basis for our understanding of the "collegial organization." If we were to call her our coauthor for this section, it would be only a slight overstatement: "Organization Culture," doctoral dissertation, Wharton School, 1982.

---

ogy product could be made in a certain way. The company's chief founder had been associated with universities and brought his scientific values to the company. He believed strongly—and still does—that excellence carries its own rewards. The basic operating principle of the company is "striving for excellence" out of a "win-win" perspective.

The nature of the work has certainly supported these views. New products are developed using state-of-the-art technology, which requires a high level of interdependence among groups and individuals. There is often a high level of uncertainty around their activities and frequent change in the technology, market, or competition. To some extent then, each product is a unique case application. The engineers value "having fun" and "being challenged" with the work they do. The environment of this particular sector of industry is highly competitive, involving large stakes; there is rapid, spasmodic growth in the careers of highly, often precociously gifted scientists and engineers.

The management of scientific and technical information is an important aspect of remaining competitive because of the nature of the task. In this company—let's refer to it as "LED"—information is often transferred through verbal, face-to-face communication, and there is a strong value that encourages information sharing.

The decision-making style is participative and encourages a "bottom-up" flow of ideas aimed at generating consensus around all issues. This means that *all* people who effect or are affected by a decision have a say in the decision. Consensus means getting no objections, the absence of undermining or interference in any given activity. It does not mean that everyone has the same opinion, idea, or strategy. It does mean that all participating members have a say—that they agree to allow some amount of time for the issue to resolve itself, prove itself, destroy itself, or whatever. This form of collegial management can be observed in all major and minor decisions confronting LED, from corporate strategy and product goals to design specifications and worker compensation.

Power, influence, and status are based on peer recognition at LED, not hierarchical position. Peer recognition, in turn, is based on how competent people are thought to be and, to a certain extent, on interpersonal skills. People are expected to fight hard for what they believe in, but to fight in an above-board, open, fair, and clean fashion.

Figure 3 illustrates LED's themes, its "collegial architecture." Where did such a culture come from? We have already intimated that LED's founder brought academic and scientific values to the company. Specifically, he had worked in a university-related government laboratory. Like so many others, he decided to go off on his own when his idea for a new device attracted little interest at the laboratory. In addition to his scientific values, the founder of LED is a deeply religious man and a highly ethical person who believes that no one, including himself, knows all the answers; that the world is a confusing, ambiguous place, with problems and predicaments so complex that the more people you could put to work on a problem, the more opportunities you would have to find a solution. He had and still retains a lot of trust in people. In the early days of the company's history, he hadn't heard of McGregor's "Theory Y" or anything like participative management, but he had his own ideas, which seemed to embody those values, and he held them very strongly.

One anecdote about the founder (no longer LED's president) involves a newly hired engineer. The recruit, who had come from a rival computer firm, told management that he had brought along some important "secrets" from the competing firm. When LED's president heard this, the story goes, he became furious and told the new recruit to "deep 6" those secrets, saying that this was the last he wanted to hear about that kind of thievery and that LED didn't do business that way.

Participative or collegial structure is gaining popularity in the United States as elsewhere. We are learning from the Japanese model and also incorporating the precepts of interpersonal psychologies. This particular structure seems particularly well suited to rapidly growing and highly competitive scientific technologies that rely on aggressive research and development divisions.

The Personalistic Style

Jordan Manufacturing is a super place. It has super profits, super policies, super products, super productivity,

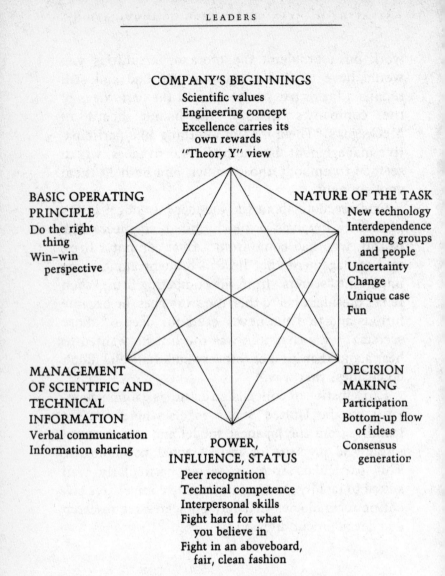

COMPANY'S BEGINNINGS
Scientific values
Engineering concept
Excellence carries its
 own rewards
"Theory Y" view

BASIC OPERATING
PRINCIPLE
Do the right
 thing
Win–win
 perspective

NATURE OF THE TASK
New technology
Interdependence
 among groups
 and people
Uncertainty
Change
Unique case
Fun

MANAGEMENT
OF SCIENTIFIC AND
TECHNICAL
INFORMATION
Verbal communication
Information sharing

POWER,
INFLUENCE, STATUS
Peer recognition
Technical competence
Interpersonal skills
Fight hard for what
 you believe in
Fight in an aboveboard,
 fair, clean fashion

DECISION
MAKING
Participation
Bottom-up flow
 of ideas
Consensus
 generation

Fig. 3. The social architecture of LED: the collegial structure. (From M. Wilkof's "Organization Culture," see footnote,
page 110.)

super potential, and the ones who make this happen—super people. But what makes the story of this company even more remarkable is that job shops are notoriously unsuper businesses. Torn asunder by labor-management divisiveness, populated by blue-collar workers in jobs that are going nowhere, and character-ized by anomie born of boredom and depersonaliza-tion, job shops are not usually the places one would look to find creative people doing top-quality work.*

This is the dramatic story of Jim Jackson, owner and founder of Jordan. When he speaks about the renaissance of the blue-collar worker, it sounds a bit like overselling—the kind of evangelical fervor that sets one's teeth on edge. But after spending some time with Jordan and talking with Jackson, we're convinced that there's more behind Jackson's man-agement style than rhetoric. Much more.

Jim bought Jordan after a long career making his way up the corporate ladder. As a boy—unlike most kids of his age, who collected baseball cards and wor-shiped sports heroes—Jim memorized the names of the presidents of the Fortune 500 companies. He wanted to be one someday. But something always got in his way. When he was passed over as CEO of one of those Fortune 500s, he dismantled his childhood dream and emerged with a new vision: He would buy

*Jordan Manufacturing is a pseudonym as is Jim Jackson. We have taken a number of liberties to protect the actual company's anonymity. Full credit, though, must be given to Sue McKibben, who wrote the case from which this section was adapted. We have also integrated material from another case with Jordan, making it appear as one case when it is actually two.

his own place and manage it the way he always wanted to be managed.

According to one of our students who studied Jordan, Jim Jackson is "bigger than life." He reminds his staff to "walk tall" with both his words and his deeds. He makes a point of going out on the shop floor at least twice a week to compliment those who have done exceptionally well, ask how things are going with the family, and check out the "climate" of the place. There's no danger that the staff will feel he's trying to second-guess them regarding how they should be performing their tasks, because he knows next to nothing about job-shop technicalities. He loves to be quoted saying that he "hardly knows how to start a car."

Jackson's competitive strategy is based on quality and service, which seems to be what everybody is talking about these days. It's quite another thing to provide them to the customer, which Jordan does. An author of a magazine article about Jordan observed that "the company's success is primarily based on a considered strategy of building trust between employees and owners."

An article in a trade publication said: "From the outset Jackson told key people the management philosophy was that 'We're going down that highway right there. If you don't understand it, yell. If you don't agree, yell, and we'll get it sorted out together.'" The vehicle for getting down that highway is Jackson's management style, embodied in an assortment of informal corporate policies. The closest we could come to a formal, explicit statement about his philosophy was a half-page bulletin he circulated shortly after buying the company:

• People want to do a good job and be associated with success!
• People will do a good job if:
    They understand the need!
    They are provided:
        Facilities and equipment
        Procedures
        Material
        Know-how
        Management that leads
    Their efforts are recognized and appreciated
    We attach no blame to "failure"
    Everybody assumes responsibility for the product
    We leave workers alone and allow them flexibility

It might be interesting to quote a few managers at Jordan to get their perceptions of Jordan and Jackson:

I have a lot of respect for Jim. Everything he told me about this place during the interview was done. No bullshit. He's stood by his word. It seemed too good to be true. I thought, "What will I actually find when I get there?" A few weeks later I asked him about something and he said, "What did I tell you?" And I thought, "OK. He's the real thing."

Here's an excerpt from an interview with another manager:

Well, the pressure's pretty intense here and there is a lot of turnover. . . .

Q. Have you ever thought about leaving?

A. Sure crossed my mind. I'm plenty frustrated but there's still so much opportunity and challenge here and we're just a damned good company.

Q. What do you do when you get frustrated?

A. Well, if I can talk with Jim, that's OK.

Q. Can you really level with him?

A. Yeah, about most things.

Q. What can't you discuss with him?

A. Well, I'm not really sure. Although he talks about delegation and encourages us to groom our people, I'm not really sure that he really grooms his "direct reports." But I have discussed that with him. . . .

Q. How do you succeed around here?

A. I'm supposed to be like Jim. You see, I grew up with the company and have had about ten years to learn, and I could adjust to the changes and respond to what's wanted and needed. I wonder what's going to happen to those new people who haven't had the opportunity to work directly with Jim.

Q. How would you describe the characteristics of the successful Jordan executive?

A. To begin with, you've got to be technically excellent; whether you're in marketing or manufacturing or whatever, you've got to be damned good in what you do. Gotta have foresight and lead clean, frugal lives. . . . Informal

BOOKS·A·MILLION

shop online at booksamillion.com

Store # 428
1866-1 East Market Street
Harrisonburg   VA 22801
540-574-4490

SKU	Description	QTY	PRICE	TOTAL
001325211 LEADERS		1	$13.50	$13.50
Original Price:	$15.00			

Sub Total		$13.50
Tax	0.00	$0.61
Total		$14.11
Check		$14.11

Do You Have A Discount Card?
Ask An Associate How To Save 10%
Everyday At Books-A-Million
Millionaire Club Savings - $1.50

Associate:Ashley   ID: 1108

Trx 8208 Str 428 Reg 01 Till:08   4/22/03 13:33

SKU	Description	QTY	PRICE	TOTAL
0013252I7 LEADERS		1	$13.50	$13.50
Original Price:	$15.00			

Sub Total			$13.50
Tax	0.00		$0.61
Total			$14.11

Check			$14.11

Associate:Ashley   ID: 1108

Trx: 8208 Str 428 Reg 01 7/17/08   4/22/03 13:33

... look at Jim. More responsibility than we can handle.... No frills, no fancy stuff. We all go coach fare. No Hiltons or Marriotts.

Q. You mean Holiday Inns?

A. Yeah—Holiday Inns and Best Western.

Q. Sounds like you're describing Jim?

A. Damn right!

When the interviewer asked a top manager at Jordan to draw a cartoon (or describe a cartoon) that would best characterize Jordan's social architecture, he said:

There's a guy with a spyglass ... that's Jim. ... He's looking at the future ... juggling a lot of balls in the air. He's on a ship, on the prow, full steam ahead, with the balls in the air and sort of looking through the spyglass. It's a decent-sized ship, going like a bat out of hell ... a destroyer, a naval destroyer. Every once in a while, the guy with the spyglass—I guess that's Jim—leaves the balls and spyglass alone and goes around and talks to the crew and kind of gets everybody to think that this particular voyage is the most important thing we can be doing. And we believe him!

When we discussed Jordan's social architecture with the company's human resources vice president (and asked her to focus on the problems there), she said that there are a number of problems. "Most likely," she said, "our biggest problem when it comes to the people side of things is that there is only a small percentage of managers who serve as role models. Also, managers 'happen,' they're not systematically developed. That's about it. But that's not trivial."

Jim Jackson likes to remind himself that Vince Lombardi used to talk about how it's "a game of inches." "I want that inch. I want that inch," he says. Jordan wins, according to Jackson, because it's a game of thousandths of an inch—a game that can only be won the hard way—considering the millions of precision parts the company makes every year. And they seem to be winning—hands down.

Jackson's goals for Jordan were and are simple: to steadily expand the company and raise profits, to share the wealth, and to enable everyone to feel satisfaction and have fun on the job. He thought that the only way to do that would be "to create an atmosphere of complete trust between us, our employees and our customers." That seems to be what's happened.

The Formalistic Style

It wasn't until the 1920s that Alfred P. Sloan hit on what was quickly to become the basic model for industrial (and other kinds of) organizations. At General Motors, Sloan combined a decentralized manufacturing system with centralized policy and financial control. In fact, the GM model—which is the archetypal formalistic one—remains as the major organizational model, not only in the United States but throughout the industrialized world.

GM, like most large, complex systems, has a formal structure that emphasizes clear-cut, explicit rules; a formal committee structure; and a clear division of labor into "finance" and "operations." The rationale for this structure was provided by Sloan's now famous 1920 document called the "Organizational Plan." Sloan said that the objective of his plan was to preserve the best features of decentralized operations while introducing a measure of financial control and interdivisional communication, which would maximize the efforts and efficiencies of the diverse and integrated companies.

> In the great expansion in General Motors between 1918 and 1920, I had been struck by the disparity between substance and form: plenty of substance and little form. I became convinced that the corporation could not continue to grow and survive unless it was better organized and it was apparent that no one was giving that subject the attention it needed.[4]

So wrote Sloan in *My Years with General Motors*, and it reflected then his frustration with the rapid, unplanned growth of GM during the first fifth of this century and his impatience with the legacy of the founder of GM, the freewheeling, imaginative, inveterate gambler William Durant. Durant wheeled and dealed GM into worldwide success and dominance in the automobile industry. His manner, though broad in scope, was sometimes capricious, leaving his associates concerned and confused. Under Durant's leadership, GM operated with no central control to speak of. His technique was the extreme example of decentralized management, one suited to his talents, because he was not an adept administrator. According to all available sources, GM under Durant was so informally managed that there was no formal accounting performed in the corporation until after Sloan urged that an annual, certified audit of the corporate books be conducted. There was no central guidance and direction for the corporation, no orderly growth plan. By 1910, Durant had enlarged GM to include twenty-five smaller companies which, for the most part, built automobile accessories. They were loosely organized, each company practically running itself. The parent firm served as a holding company.

When the 1920 recession hit, GM was overstocked in inventory (because of Durant's entrepreneurial lust; his eye for expansion took in more than he could afford) and overbuilt in product for the slowing marketplace. GM was out of control and had to borrow $83 million in short-term notes to meet its current obligations. Under pressure, Durant resigned from GM on November 20, 1920.*

Amid this turmoil and floundering in 1920, Sloan, then President Pierre Du Pont's top lieutenant, was displaying his prodigious talents as a financial and

---

*He died, as he was born, practically a pauper, on March 18, 1947. His last working days were spent managing a bowling alley in Flint, Michigan. It was said to be typical of Durant that in his last business days he wasn't so much concerned with running the bowling alley as he was with laying plans for fifty bowling centers to be built across the country.

organizational genius. His "Organizational Plan" was and still is one of the most important statements on organizational management. He said that the objective of his plan was to preserve the best features of decentralized operations while introducing a measure of financial control and interdivisional communication, which would maximize the efforts and efficiencies of the company. The proposal had two broad principles:

1. The responsibility attached to the chief executive of each operation shall in no way be limited. Each such organization headed by its chief executive shall be complete in every necessary function and enabled to exercise its full initiative and logical development.
2. Certain central organizational functions are absolutely essential to the logical development and proper control of the corporation's activities.[5]

Sloan was fully aware of the contradiction inherent in those two principles. He also realized that in order for the plan to work, a delicate balance would have to be maintained between the freedom of the various operations (Durant's style) to manage their own activities and the controls necessary to coordinate these operations. What's most important to keep in mind is that the "Organizational Plan" laid down a definite formal organizational arrangement for the "once and future" GM and established the social architecture that managed successfully to braid the entrepreneurial adventurism of Durant with the tal-

ents of a brilliant operations executive, embodied by
Sloan himself.

As the GM culture emerged under Sloan's shadow,
according to most reports, a dominant theme began
to emerge as characteristic of that culture. This
theme was central to the management philosophy at
GM and included the following core values: respect-
ing authority, "fitting in," and loyalty.

One of the most common cultural expressions of
deference due to the men holding high-status positions was the use of a special language or jargon to
refer to the domain of these executives. Their offices
were located in one I-shaped end of the fourteenth
floor of the huge GM headquarters building.
Employees referred to it as "The Fourteenth Floor"
and "Executive Row." In his book on the John Z.
DeLorean days at GM, *On a Clear Day You Can See
General Motors*, J. Patrick Wright wrote, "In General
Motors the words 'The Fourteenth Floor' are spoken
with reverence."[6] Their high status was clearly
reflected in the physical layout of the fourteenth
floor. The entrance to this floor was a boundary,
designed in part to communicate the difficulty of
gaining entrance into these hallowed halls:

> . . . a thick glass door protects the entrance to
> The Fourteenth Floor. It is electronically locked
> and is opened by a receptionist who actuates a
> switch under her desk in a large, plain waiting
> room outside the door.

Once inside, the eerie silence reinforced an impres-
sion of great power:

. . . The atmosphere on The Fourteenth Floor is awesomely quiet. The hallways are usually deserted. People speak in hushed voices. The omnipresent quiet projects an aura of great power. The reason it is so quiet must mean that General Motors' powerful executives are hard at work in their offices studying problems, analyzing mountains of complicated data, holding meetings and making important, calculated business decisions. There is no room for laughter or casual conversations in the halls. Those are frivolous. There is too much work to be done to be frivolous.[7]

As far as "fitting in" goes, evidence was everywhere to be seen, in the way employees dressed, in the way their offices were decorated, in the lifestyles they chose. The dress code in the sixties consisted of a dark suit, a light shirt, and a muted, possibly striped tie.

In the first chapter of Wright's book, John Z. DeLorean reveals "Why I Quit General Motors":

And I thought about what I felt was a tragic irony of my resignation: That this mammoth corporation, which was founded by a maverick, Billy Durant, and built into the prototype of the well-run American business by men who were distinct individuals, could not today accept or accommodate an executive who had made his mark in the corporation by being different and individualistic. I never pretended to compare myself with the great founders and shapers of the modern General Motors—Alfred P. Sloan, Jr., the Du Pont family, Donaldson Brown and others. But I was a student of their techniques, and it bothered me that I was no longer able to work for the company that they had founded. . . . There was no place for me.[8]

It doesn't take a genius to discern almost immediately the contrast between the formal, clear-cut, and explicit social architecture of GM and the almost Durantean entrepreneurial spirit of Jordan Manufacturing. Or the contrast with LED's collegiality, for that matter. And when one considers DeLorean's "exit" statement just quoted, it becomes clear that he, too, understood with accuracy (and at the same time violated) the unwritten but sacred canon of GM which we refer to as its style of social architecture.

Even the most unreflective person would have a difficult time overlooking the contrasting styles of social architecture in the three organizations we have described. Jim Jackson would find the fourteenth floor at GM unbearably stifling. And neither LED's founder nor Sloan, for that matter, would be comfortable at Jordan Manufacturing. To sum up, with LED and its *collegial* style, the dominant emphasis is on consensus, on peer-group membership, on teamwork. Under Jackson's leadership, the social architecture's dominant theme is *personalistic*; at its extreme, a legitimized anarchy, where the locus of decision making is within each individual. GM represents the other extreme, a *formalistic* culture, where behavior is derived from explicit rules and policies and where deviation from the rules is questionable at best and heretical at worst.

We can safely say that these three styles of social architecture account for roughly 95 percent of contemporary organizations. Of those we're most familiar with, some leading candidates for the *formalistic* style can be selected from any of the following: AT&T, Procter & Gamble, Pacific Telesis, Bank of America, Imperial Chemical Industries, Ford Motor Company, the Los Angeles Dodgers, Times-Mirror, Inc., the State Department, most regulated industries, and many more from among the Fortune 500 companies. *Collegial* organizations are frequently found in the high-tech sector, in many partnership organizations, and where there is a high proportion of professional employees. The Silicon Valley and the Route 128 area (outside of Boston) abound with examples. Such firms as Intel, Digital, Data General, and Hewlett-Packard are archetypal. So is Arthur D. Little, the consulting firm, or TRW, even with its heavy manufacturing bias. And even a bank such as Citicorp qualifies.

Many a "young" entrepreneurial, high-growth organization—often the brainchild of an inventor-founder—turns out to be *personalistic*. Examples such as Gore-Tex, Thompson Vitamins, the Foothill Group, the Hotel Corporation of America, the Louisville Cardinals and The Limited come to mind. (As they "age," however, many personalistic organizations have a tendency to move either toward a collegial or formalistic type of social architecture.)

The following table identifies the major themes of the three styles of architecture and may help the reader see where his or her organization stands in this respect.

To sum up, we have drawn careful distinctions between three forms of social architecture, each consistent within itself and each capable of being enormously successful when properly deployed. The leader, as social architect, must be part artist, part designer, part master craftsman, facing the challenge of aligning the elements of the social architecture so that, like an ideal building, it becomes a creative synthesis uniquely suited to realizing the guiding vision of the leader.

Social architecture, as we have continually emphasized, provides *meaning*. The key point is that if an organization is to be transformed, the social architecture must be revamped. The effective leader needs to articulate new values and norms, offer new visions, and use a variety of tools in order to transform, support, and institutionalize new meanings and directions. Let's turn to that in our final section.

TOOLS OF THE SOCIAL ARCHITECT

... the most successful leader of all is one who sees another picture not yet actualized. He sees the things which belong in his present picture but which are not yet there. ... Above all, he should make his co-workers see that it is not *his* purpose which is to be achieved, but a common purpose, born of the desires and the activities of the group.

Mary Parker Follett[9]

A burning question is whether an organization can deliberately change its social architecture. After all,

Table 1 THREE STYLES OF SOCIAL ARCHITECTURE

Values/Behavior	Formalistic	Collegial	Personalistic
Basis for decision	Direction from authority	Discussion, agreement	Directions from within
Forms of control	Rules, laws, rewards, punishments	Interpersonal, group commitments	Actions aligned with self-concept
Source of power	Superior	What "we" think and feel	What I think and feel
Desired end	Compliance	Consensus	Self-actualization
To be avoided	Deviation from authoritative direction; taking risks	Failure to reach consensus	Not being "true to oneself"
Position relative to others	Hierarchical	Peer	Individual
Human relationships	Structured	Group-oriented	Individually oriented
Basis for growth	Following the established order	Peer group membership	Acting on awareness of self

we have to ask: Just how tractable are such features as shared values, commitments, decision processes and so on? Although there are no easy answers to this question and certainly no "cookbook recipes" for such fundamental changes, there are several examples that we can point to and learn from. Lee Iacocca's experience at Chrysler is one. He created a new vision, mobilized the work force behind that vision and worked toward solidifying the commitment for the changes he brought about. Louis Gerstner of IBM, with a style much different than that of Iacocca, has been working to develop a new mission and culture at that firm. When IBM's mainframe and minicomputer sales nose-dived in the early 1990s, it seemed paralyzed, unable to decide where its priorities lay. Shortly after he arrived in 1993, Gerstner replaced many old-line managers, abandoned the venerable IBM dress code, placed a new emphasis on growing the service unit, and announced a deluge of new products and technological alliances designed to transform the company. Such actions are also under way at AT&T, Chase Manhattan Bank, Apple Computer, United Airlines and a host of other leading corporations.

What we've learned about transforming social architecture comes directly from the experiences of the leaders we interviewed. For a successful transformation to be achieved, three things have to happen—and these principles *apply equally to each and every one* of the three styles just described:

1. Create a new and compelling vision capable of bringing the workforce to a new place.
2. Develop commitment for the new vision.
3. Institutionalize the new vision.*

Create a New Vision

The effective leader must assemble for the organization a vision of a desired future state. While this task may be shared and developed with other key members of the organization, it remains the core responsibility and cannot be delegated. At General Electric, developing the new vision was the direct responsibility of Jack Welch, and while it took a great amount of staff work, it was shaped by Welch's philosophy and style. Iacocca relied more on his instincts than on staff reports and was personally aggressive in developing a new vision and mission. The point is that the transformation of social architecture must begin at the top of the organization with the CEO and have the full support of the board and the inner circle of top officers. The CEO whose behavior is consistent with the norms and values he or she has articulated for the organization has an enormous head start.

AT&T provides an apt illustration here. Several years before the process of divestiture began, Chairman Charles L. Brown began to set the stage for

*The work of Noel Tichy has been especially valuable to us in this section.[2]

transformation in a number of speeches. In one of his most important addresses, before the Commercial Club of Chicago, Mr. Brown asserted:

> ... there is a new telephone company in town ... a high-technology business applying advanced marketing strategies to the satisfaction of highly sophisticated customer requirements. ... "Ma Bell" is no longer an appropriate name for this company ... Mother doesn't live here anymore.[11]

AT&T had a new mission, and as Bell's employees began to think of themselves as "competitive" rather than "regulated," the managerial focus shifted to the marketplace.

Of course, the AT&T transformation took a lot of time and many detours, and it is still not complete. It has survived waves of layoffs, a disastrous foray into the computer field and powerful new competitors in its core long-distance business. Although no one doubts that AT&T is a more viable and aggressive competitor today, it is clear that the long-term challenge to revitalizing social architecture (and an assessment of its success) has less to do with how the vision is created and more with the extent to which the vision correctly *positions* the organization in its competitive environment. (The following chapter will be entirely devoted to "positioning the organization.")

Develop Commitment for the New Vision

The organization must be mobilized to accept and support the new vision—to make it happen. One of the presidents we interviewed took his top 900 executives on a five-day retreat to share and discuss the vision. Of course, it doesn't take five days to share one short mission statement and eight objectives. But commitment requires more than verbal compliance, more than just dialogue and exchange. At the least, the vision has to be articulated clearly and frequently in a variety of ways, from "statements of policy" that have minimum impact to revising recruiting aims and methods, training that is explicitly geared to modify behavior in support of new organizational values, and, not the least, adapting and modifying shared symbols that signal and reinforce the new vision.

Regarding the last, the use of symbols, AT&T is an interesting case. It did lose the Bell name and the logo, which then afforded it an opportunity to reinforce Mr. Brown's message, both internally and externally, that "Ma Bell doesn't live here anymore." AT&T continued to use AT&T as its trade name, thereby capitalizing on its long-standing reputation throughout the world. It replaced the familiar logo (a bell within a circle) with a globe symbolically girdled by electronic communications. Thus AT&T has a new symbol, which, according to its publicity, "suggests new dimensions—of our business and our future."[12]

After the leader creates a vision and mobilizes

commitment, perhaps the most difficult challenge begins, that of institutionalizing the new vision and mission.

Institutionalize the New Vision

There is a story about Sun-tzu, a great Chinese general, who lived two and a half thousand years ago. The king ordered Sun-tzu to train his army, and the general, after drilling and disciplining them to his satisfaction, asked the king to inspect his troops. But the king replied that he didn't want to, whereupon Sun-tzu said calmly, "The king is only fond of words and cannot translate them into deeds."[13] Words, symbols, articulation, training and recruiting, while necessary, don't go far enough. Changes in the management processes, organizational structure, and management style all must support the changes in the pattern of values and behavior that a new vision implies.

To take one vivid illustration, the basic job of restructuring postdivestiture AT&T involved a move from its former geographical profit-center orientation to a national line-of-business profit-center orientation. To implement this significant change, AT&T immediately had to redeploy 13,000 employees from corporate staff to the prospective postdivestiture division or subsidiary staffs. And the remaining cadre of AT&T executives who remained at corporate headquarters were reorganized around a policy/strategy/financial-management framework appropriate for the new market-based businesses.

Nor is this a one-time process. At AT&T, as at most companies, aligning the organization with a new vision is a continuing process as the vision takes hold. At AT&T, tens of thousands of jobs were cut in the mid-1980s and even more in the 1990s. The company invested billions of dollars in computers, acquiring and then spinning off a failing NCR; delayed investing in cellular phones and then paid a small fortune for McCaw Cellular; spun off its communications development and manufacturing operations into a new firm called Lucent Technologies; and made other massive alterations. Each time, the entire organization had to be reconfigured.

Translating intention into reality is what we're getting at here. And that involves not only organizational mission, structure and human resource systems but also the political and cultural forces that drive the system. Until Lee Iacocca took over as leader of Chrysler, the basic internal political structure had remained unchanged for years. One of Iacocca's first acts was to redefine Chrysler's links to various external stakeholders, not only to the government, which was lobbied successfully to guarantee substantial loans, but to the UAW as well, by inviting UAW president Douglas Fraser to join the Chrysler board.

Iacocca was equally impressive in the cultural realm. He had to change the cultural values from a "losers" to a "winners" feeling. That was particularly difficult not only because of Chrysler's spotty past performance but because of the stigma attached to being "bailed out" by the government. And this change had to be accomplished with fewer resources than Chrysler's competitors had. This Iacocca achieved, visibly and forcefully, by his frequent messages to the workers and, perhaps more important, by his own personal appearances in Chrysler ads to reinforce his internal messages. Over a period of a year or two, the internal culture was transformed to that of a lean and hungry team looking for victory—and competent enough to achieve it.[14]

CHANGING THE SOCIAL ARCHITECTURE

The leader is an effective social architect to the extent that he can manage meaning. We've said that throughout. Doing that, however, seems to be both obvious and mysterious. But if there is one lesson that emerges from our analysis of the best practices in this complex area, it appears to stem from leaders doing a lot of fairly simple and obvious things well. This is said in no way to minimize or trivialize the difficulties in mastering social architecture, but in retrospect it does seem that our effective leaders all apply common sense.

In the case of Lee Iacocca, it was his brio and confidence and getting his message across to the public (and indirectly to his troops) that made the difference. AT&T not only changed its logo but also transformed its operations completely, from a geographical profit-center orientation to a national line-of-business profit-center orientation. Many companies bring in a new CEO to transform the social architecture. According to Jim Burke, former chairman and CEO of Johnson & Johnson, perhaps the world's most successful health-care company, there are and were a number of factors that shaped the organization's social architecture. Both he and Robert Wood Johnson, "the General," son of the founder and former chairman of the company, shared a belief that "if you have sensible people who know each other, in a small enough group, somehow or other problems would get worked out."[15] Given General Johnson's and Jim Burke's strong convictions about the inherent superiority of small, autonomous units, decentralization became a major strategic direction for the company. But Burke also recognizes and acknowledges the influence of the Credo, which, for the most part, reflected and formalized the General's views on public and social responsibility. Burke described the influence of the Credo on J&J managers as follows:

All of our management is geared to profit on a day-by-day basis. That's part of the business of being in business. But too often, in this and other businesses, people are inclined to think, "We'd better do this because if we don't, it's going to show up on the figures over the short term." This document allows them to say, "Wait a minute. I don't have to do that. The management has told me that they're really interested in the long term, and they're interested in me operating under this set of principles. So I won't."[16]

But Burke was quick to add that it's not one single thing that creates and sustains a particular social architecture. Notwithstanding the universal acknowledgment accorded the Credo within J&J, Burke perceived some degree of tokenism and a need to inculcate within the managers the values underlying this statement. He described his actions thus:

People like my predecessor believed the Credo with a passion, but the operating unit managers were not universally committed to it. There seemed to be a growing attitude that it was there but that nobody had to do anything about it. So I called a meeting of some twenty key executives and challenged them. I said, "Here's the Credo. If we're not going to live by it, let's tear it off the wall. If you want to change it, tell us how to change it. We either ought to commit to it or get rid of it."

The meeting was a turn-on, because we were challenging people's own personal values. By the end of the session, the managers had gained a great deal of understanding about and enthusiasm for the beliefs in the Credo. Subsequently, Dave Clare and I have met with small groups of J&J managers all over the world to challenge the Credo.

Now, I don't really think that you can impose convictions or beliefs on someone else. However, I do believe that if I really understand what makes the business work, then I can prompt you to think through the facts and come to see just how pragmatic the philosophy is when it comes to running a business successfully. . . . And I think that's what happened here.[17]

For many, including J&J managers, the strongest evidence of the Credo's power was witnessed in the company's response to the Tylenol crisis. Their response prompted the *Washington Post* to write that "Johnson & Johnson has succeeded in portraying itself to the public as a company willing to do what's right, regardless of cost."[18]

At Intel, the mosaic of elements that shape and sustain the social architecture are as diverse *and* as simple and complex as J&J's. Among other things, Intel's social architecture includes a strong "university program" where over eighty courses are taught, taken, and paid for exclusively by Intel employees, from the chairman to the shop employees. Andy Grove, the president, for example, created and still teaches a course called "Creative Confrontation," a course that pretty much sums up Grove's leadership philosophy and the company's culture. One of the authors of this book was retained as a consultant to help Intel develop a course on leadership. Before the course was initiated, the entire top-management group took the course directly from the author at a two-day, off-site retreat and then spent a few months ironing out the bugs they detected when they were the author's students. Now they offer it themselves.

And then there are Andy Grove's informal and "colorful" memos that he sends out sporadically. Whoever receives them, whether they are positive or negative, usually posts them in a prominent place for everyone to see. One of the first "Andy-grams" the author noticed was a letter written by a top executive to Grove and returned by Grove to the sender with a large red stamp over the entire letter which said: *BULLSHIT!* DO IT AGAIN!

Jim Burke used his executive committee. William McGowan, former head of MCI, talked endlessly to anyone he bumped into—a clear example of Peters and Waterman's "management by wandering around." Some leaders "show" and others "tell." In no case did one of our effective leaders delegate the task of shaping social architecture to anyone else. Nor did we find one effective leader whose activities, when it comes to influencing the social architecture, ever run down or abate.

The metamorphosis that is involved in the transformation of the social architecture of any organization—no matter how small or large, no matter what style of social architecture is dominant—"would challenge the most boastful caterpillar."[19] The organizational, operational, and technological complexities to be faced are enormous. In our view, it remains as the most difficult task facing management today. All the same, mature organizations must revitalize one way or another in order to compete in increasingly tough environments. And transforming these institutions requires a special brand of leadership that we are not only advocating but deem necessary if our organizations are to achieve their goals.

STRATEGY III: TRUST THROUGH POSITIONING

Fail to honor people,
They fail to honor you;
But of a good leader, who talks little,
When his work is done, his aim fulfilled,
They will all say, "We did this ourselves."

Lao-tzu

When Frank Dale took over as publisher of the *Los Angeles Herald-Examiner*, the organization had just ended a ten-year strike. There was much bitterness and, as he told us, "Everybody that I found there had lost their curiosity, they'd lost their cutting edge, there was no interest, they just hung on. . . . I had a real problem." His very first task was to introduce himself to everybody, to thank them for their loyalty to that point, and to allow them to express their concerns and frustrations. To questions like "What makes you think you can make this thing go?" he responded, "I don't know yet, but in thirty days I'll come back to you and let you know what I've found." He recruited a task force of the best people from throughout the Hearst Corporation to do a crash study, and in thirty days he had a written report on what needed to be done, which he shared with the staff. He had taken the all-important first steps to establish mutual trust, without which leadership would not have been possible.

Trust is the emotional glue that binds followers and leaders together. The accumulation of trust is a measure of the legitimacy of leadership. It cannot be mandated or purchased; it must be earned. Trust is the basic ingredient of all organizations, the lubrication that maintains the organization, and, as we said earlier, it is as mysterious and elusive a concept as leadership—and as important.

One thing we can say for sure about trust is that if trust is to be generated, there must be *predictability*, the capacity to predict another's behavior. Another way of putting it is to say that organizations without trust would resemble the ambiguous nightmare of Kafka's *The Castle*, where nothing can be certain and nobody can be relied on or be held accountable. The ability to predict outcomes with a high probability of success generates and maintains trust.

In organizational settings of the kind we have been discussing, trust between leaders and followers cannot exist without two conditions:

- The leader's *vision* for the organization must be clear, attractive, and attainable. We tend to trust leaders who create these visions, since vision represents the context for shared beliefs in a common organizational purpose.
- The leader's *positions* must be clear. We tend to trust leaders when we know where they stand in relation to the organization and how they position the organization relative to the environment.

Vision and position stand in the same relationship to each other as do thought and action or an idea and its enactment. Vision, of course, is also the main catalyst in the management of attention, which we discussed in the chapter on Strategy I. This chapter will focus on *positioning*, the most complex and least understood aspect in the management of trust. But its importance cannot be exaggerated: it is the organizational reciprocal of vision, that which animates and inspirits the leader's vision.

In the next section, we will define as precisely as we can positioning and its role in organizational effectiveness. Following that we will introduce a practical and original method for building trust. In conclusion, we will draw lessons for the leader's role in positioning the organization.

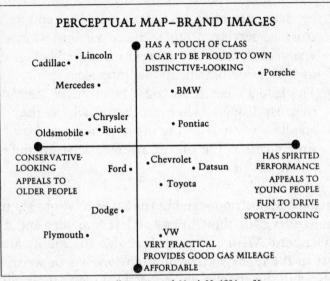

Source: Chrysler Corp.   *Wall Street Journal*, March 22, 1984, p. 35.

Fig. 4 Product positioning.

ORGANIZATIONS AND THEIR
ENVIRONMENTS

Marketing managers have long been familiar with the notion of product positioning. An automobile company, for example, might map its products as shown in Figure 4. By doing so, it defines a distinctive niche in the marketplace and knows how to target its styling, price and advertising. At the same time, its employees, customers, managers and stockholders know what the product stands for and what the company is trying to do.

If we broaden this concept of product positioning to one of organizational positioning, we may be able to explain much of leadership behavior. "Organizational positioning" refers to the process by which an organization designs, establishes and sustains a viable niche in its external environments. It encompasses everything the leader must do to align the internal and external environments of the organization over time and space.

We can illustrate this concept with a well-known and successful company, KFC (formerly Kentucky Fried Chicken). In the past several decades, the convergence of many environmental forces such as more job opportunities for women, increased divorce rates, higher cost of living, and smaller families caused a great increase in the number of single-person households and two-wage-earner families. Recognizing that these people had little time for cooking, the leaders of the company defined a niche—the need for an inexpensive, freshly prepared, dependable meal that could be purchased and served quickly with little fuss. The company positioned all aspects of its organization for this niche—a unique *product* based on inexpensive raw materials and a distinctive flavor; a *production process* using cheap labor and standardized equipment and procedures to ensure a fast, dependable product each time; a *purchasing* system designed for enormous economies of scale with tight quality control to guarantee consistency; a *distribution* system based on thousands of small outlets conveniently located and easily recognizable; and a *management* structure suited to centralized finance, promotion, and purchasing coupled with highly decentralized production and sales. In short, what goes on inside the KFC organization is ideally positioned against the needs of its external environments.

This concept of organizational positioning applies equally to all sorts of organizations—Avis Rent-a-Car, the Boston Pops, the Boy Scouts, a local teenage hangout, or the USC Business School. Moreover, there is a strong analogy between human organizations and other organisms in this regard. Each must find an appropriate environmental niche within which to function and grow. Abrupt environmental change can cause the death of an organization just as easily as it can for any other organism that has insufficient time to adapt. The bankruptcy courts are littered with examples.

However, there are some differences between human organizations and other organisms in this regard. The first is that the environments of organizations are much *more complex* than natural environments because they contain both physical and man-made elements. In contrast to physical environments, man-made elements tend to be irregular, nonrecurring, irrational, and unpredictable. In addition, an organization must interact not only with its primary environments—such as suppliers, consumers, and interfacing organizations—but also with many technological, legal, social, economic, and institutional structures that constrain the activities of the organization and over which it has very little direct control. Table 2 lists some of the typical primary and

Table 2 DESCRIPTIONS OF AN ORGANIZATION'S EXTERNAL ENVIRONMENT

Environments	Corporation	University	Hospital	Public Agency
Primary Environments				
1. Suppliers	Banks Labor unions Suppliers of goods and services	High schools Professors Publishers Labor markets Donors, funding agencies Suppliers	Insurance companies Doctors Labor markets Donors Suppliers	Taxpayers Public employees Suppliers of goods and services Politicians
2. Consumers	Customers Stockholders	Students Patients Research community Alumni Employers	General public Research community	Service recipients Private sector
3. Interfacing organizations	Competitors Ad agencies Auditors Regulating agencies Consultants	Professional societies Alumni Media Banks Accrediting organizations Board of trustees	Medical profession Teaching hospitals Board of directors Volunteer groups Health insurance Drug companies	Other agencies Education community Consultants Citizens groups Legislators Courts Polling organizations

Secondary Environments

1. Technological	Product technologies Production technologies Research community Patents	State-of-the-art of academic discipline Educational delivery systems Computers	Medical technology Administrative systems Pharmacology	Administrative systems Research community Communications technologies
2. Political/legal	Tax laws Lobbying Subsidies and regulations	Public scholarships Federal courts Copyright laws Tenure	Medicare system Deductibility of health costs FDA Licensing agencies	Enabling legislation Court decisions Incumbent politicians
3. Social	Public attitudes Consumerism Demographic factors	Public attitudes Demographic factors Status of degrees	Public attitudes Health fads Environmentalism	Public attitudes Special interests Needs of client groups—poor, aged, etc.
4. Economic	International trade Domestic business climate Market forces Interest rates	Faculty salaries Domestic business climate Inflation Employment	Health-care costs Domestic business climate	Domestic business conditions Budgets Global economy
5. Institutional	Industry structure Trade practices Auditing standards Securities markets	Academic marketplace Admissions tests Alumni groups Athletic conferences	Nursing homes Academic medicine Public sanitation HMOs	Media practices Public hearings Committee structures Authority

secondary environments for four different kinds of organizations—a business firm, a university, a hospital and a government agency.

The second difference between human organizations and other organisms is the central importance of the *time dimension*. In most natural systems, change occurs very slowly and is often measured in thousands of years. In human systems, change can occur very rapidly. As a result, nothing is more important to modern organizations than their effectiveness in coping with change. And this leads to the third difference. Whereas other organisms change as a result of natural selection, organizations change as a result of specific choices that they make themselves. In fact, the positioning decisions of an organization are very much concerned with the *design* of an appropriate niche. In a very real sense, the organization itself chooses all of the primary environments and many of the secondary environments with which it must deal. For example, in designing its niche, KFC made a multitude of environmental choices, such as:

- The particular consumer groups it wished to serve and the rules governing their interaction
- The types of suppliers with which it would do business and the terms of the relationship
- Geographic location of outlets
- The types of media, labor markets, technologies and so on with which the company would interact

These three dimensions—complexity, the time horizon and choice—that differentiate human organizations from other organisms are the very factors with which leaders are primarily concerned in positioning their organizations.

Listen to Don Gevirtz, former chairman and CEO of the Foothill Group, an innovative asset-based lending institution, talk about positioning:

> One of the reasons our company has grown is because we've found a niche and we've constantly tried to widen that niche in the marketplace. The best example is when we sent a young MBA out to an oil patch and he lived in the oil patch. He put on hip boots and dressed like the wildcat oil drillers out there and for four months he went around to the little banks and to the independent drillers spending full time finding out what it was they needed. As a result of that study we started the energy resources division of our company, which lends money to independent drillers and all the peripheral service companies to those drillers. Those people can't borrow money from banks because banks don't want to take those kinds of risks. So we created a very, very important profit center by just taking the niche we had in general and making it a little larger, but specializing. So I believe strongly in innovation in the marketplace by finding out what your market wants and needs and what the competition does and doesn't do and finding out how to give

it to them better. I call that the concentration decision.

What Gevirtz calls "the concentration decision," we call positioning—that is, he had to position an entire new division for the new environment in which he had chosen to operate: the "oil patch." He needed a product line suited to it, managers trained in the problems of the energy field, offices located near the borrowers, and an information system to keep track of a new kind of collateral. However it's talked about, "positioning" involves creating a niche in a complex, changing environment that's unique, important, and appropriate for the resources and capabilities of an organization. How positioning is achieved may be the most important factor determining an organization's effectiveness.

There are four main strategies that leaders choose (sometimes unwittingly) in order to position their organization:

1: *Reactive.* With this approach, the organization waits for change and reacts—after the fact. Some leaders who operate in this fashion act through default, as those in the steel industry have done. In other, possibly more effective cases, a reactive strategy is designed to keep options open and to provide the necessary flexibility to cope with a wide range of occurrences. One reactive firm, a utility company, built a plant that could operate with many different kinds of fuel rather than having to rely solely on oil. A reactive mode is the least expensive (and often the most shortsighted) strategy; it may occasionally work, but only in slowly changing environments that allow enough lead time to react. We know of very few, if any, business environments possessing such lassitude as that to which the virtual death of the U.S. stereo industry gives silent testimony. Nor did any of our ninety leaders take refuge in the reactive mode. Listen to Gevirtz again:

> The concentration decision has several meanings that we teach and that we lead by in the company. The first one is that every year we ask ourselves, "What business are we in?" Well, the business that we are in is to lend money on a collaterized basis to small and medium-sized companies in the U.S. Each year we ask ourselves, "Are there any other opportunities that have presented themselves to us? Should we acquire an insurance company? Should we go into some other kind of lending? Should we become consumer lenders?" And each year our concentration decision has been that we will continue to be collateralized lenders to small companies. So that's the "What business are you in" decision.

Gevirtz's approach both illustrates and serves as an introduction to the second strategy:

2: *Change the internal environment.* Rather than waiting for change to happen to them, leaders can develop effective forecasting procedures to anticipate change and then "proact" rather than react. In the short run, they can reposition the organization by granting or withholding funds, manpower or facilities to parts of the organization expected to be affected by the changes. The toy industry routinely treats orders received from January to March as forecasts of Christmas sales and gears ordering and production to the forecasts before any consumer reaction is known.

In the long run, internal environments can be changed in a more enduring way by altering internal organizational structures; by training and education; by selection, hiring and firing; and by deliberate efforts to design a corporate culture that develops certain values at the expense of others, as discussed in the prior chapter. The securities industry is now in the middle of one of these historic restructurings. New corporate cultures are being created in anticipation of much more competitive conditions in the future deriving from new competencies (e.g., mutual funds supermarkets, on-line trading); new operating procedures (e.g., check writing and cash management accounts); and broadened international access (e.g., country funds, global underwriting).

3: *Change the external environment.* This approach requires that the organization anticipating change act upon the environment itself to make the change congenial to its needs, much as the opening movement of a symphony creates an environment that is receptive to the later movements. This might be done through advertising and lobbying efforts, collaboration with other organizations, creating new marketing niches through entrepreneurship and innovation, and various other means. Consider, for example, how a labor union may change the environment of its members by striking, how a land developer may seek changes in the zoning laws to improve a project's payoff, or how, to use Gevirtz as an example again, he's lobbied for tax reforms that would help small businesses.

4: *Establish a new linkage between the external and internal environments.* Using this mechanism, an organization anticipating change will attempt to establish a new relationship between its internal environments and anticipated external environments. In the short run, this can be done by bargaining and negotiation, where both the internal and external environments change to accommodate each other more effectively (e.g., when a company agrees with a union to improve working conditions in exchange for a long-term no-strike agreement). In the long run, the organization can establish new linkages through vertical integration, mergers and acquisitions, or innovative systems design. For example, the federal government established an Environmental Protection Agency to establish new linkages with industry and the general public, and oil companies often establish joint ventures with foreign governments. In the latter case, the joint venture represents a new form of organization for the oil company having some aspects of the public sector (e.g., preferred tax rates or access to resources) and some aspects of the private sector (e.g., private investment), which makes it better able to operate in the foreign context.

We have provided this background on positioning to set the stage for the next section, where we will introduce a practical method with which a leader can begin to build trust in an organization. This method, called QUEST (which stands for Quick Environmental Scanning Technique), is a process that permits leaders, managers, and planners in an organization to share views about future external environments that have critical implications for the organization's positioning. Then, based upon this "environmental scanning" process, it is possible to choose the high-priority options available for positioning the organization. In doing so, all the other factors contributing to trust—integrity, mutual respect, reliability, competence, and vision—are brought into play. But more about that later; for now, let's look in on a hypothetical QUEST session.

QUEST FOR POSITION

The scene was a comfortable conference room in a resort hotel. Fifteen executives of a major airline—call it Global Airways—had been brought together for a QUEST program by the president of the airline.

As the meeting was about to start, the president looked around the room and thought about the people who had gathered. He looked at the ten members of the management team and wondered how some of them, the old-timers in particular, would react. He had also invited a few of the more creative and promising younger executives—one from marketing, another from the research department, and a third from a recently acquired subsidiary. Three "outsiders" were there—a trusted airline industry consultant, an account executive from their advertising agency, and a lawyer who had formerly been a member of the FAA in Washington.

The president called the meeting to order. He expressed concern about the many changes taking place in the airline industry as a result of technological advances in aircraft, competition from new non-unionized airlines, and changing consumer attitudes toward flying. He hoped that, together, they might be able to come up with some new directions for Global Airways. He asked people to put aside their day-to-day operating concerns and to think out loud with him about longer-range opportunities and risks. He wanted them to be open, participative, and creative and to have fun doing it. He then turned the floor over to his planning director, Walter Poulson.

Poulson reviewed the QUEST process for the group. This day, he said, would be spent in wide-ranging speculation about the forces shaping the future of Global Airways and their interrelationships. Later he would analyze the work of the group and prepare three to five scenarios reflecting their views of how the future environment could unfold. Then, after everyone had a chance to read the report, they would get together again to discuss implications of the scenarios for the company.

To stimulate their imaginations, Poulson briefly reviewed some of the futures literature—Alvin Toffler's *Third Wave*, John Naisbitt's *Megatrends*, Peter F. Drucker's *Managing for the Future: The 1990's and Beyond*, Charles Handy's *The Age of*

Paradox, and others. Their views ranged from simple extrapolation of current trends or "business as usual" to expectations of very radical societal transformation as a result of major shifts in technology, values and lifestyles.

Poulson asked the group to help bound the discussion. Some thought they should look at the entire travel and tourism industry, but they finally decided to concentrate on the airline business and its immediate supporting activities. Some thought they should restrict their attention to the next five years or so because of the dramatic changes in the industry, but one of the vice presidents pointed out that any major positioning decision—such as new facilities, fleet configurations, or routing—would take many years to implement and might not even be in place until after the year 2005. They agreed to focus on the years in which these decisions would have their greatest payoffs (e.g., 2010–2020). One of the line executives remarked, "I don't know what's going to happen next week, let alone fifteen years from now." The president replied that no one can predict what *will* happen, but certainly this group was knowledgeable enough to identify most of the things that *could* happen, and this would provide useful guidance in assessing the risk of setting off in a new direction.

Poulson next had the participants list the company's "stakeholders"—those individuals or groups that could affect or would be affected by the future actions of Global Airways. The group quickly named over twenty stakeholders, which he duly recorded on a large sheet of paper. They included passengers, employees, stockholders, competitors, the federal government, state and local interests, the management of the airline, its bankers, and even, as one participant pointed out, "my wife." When all the stakeholders were listed, a vote showed that the three most important were the passengers, the employees, and the stockholders. One by one, Poulson asked what each major stakeholder would like to have Global Airways do (or be prevented from doing) in the next two decades. A long list was soon developed—for example, for "passengers," it included such items as high quality of service, safety, low fares, schedule dependability, convenience and comfort.

After a coffee break, the group discussed indicators of performance. Poulson's question was, "If you were to come back in twenty years and wanted to understand the position of Global Airways and measure its success over the intervening years, what would you inquire about?" Some thirty indicators were suggested, including measures of profitability, efficiency, financial risk, employee relationships, market satisfaction and safety records. The group picked the five most important measures, which were to provide the basis, later, for evaluating the various positioning options available to the organization.

Poulson then posed the following question: "What are the critical events that could happen between now and the year 2020 which, if they did occur, would greatly impact upon the viability of Global Airways? In other words, I want us to think about those developments which are important for us to pay attention to, even if they don't now seem to have a high probability. Let's first think about developments that could occur that would affect the structure and competition in the airline industry." This led to a spirited discussion in which forty-five developments were identified, including those listed below.

Some Developments That Can Affect
Competition or Industry Structure

1. Placing of limits on flights from certain airports
2. National unionization of pilots
3. Expansion of unionization to cover skills and trades not currently unionized
4. Modernization of a major airline carrier's fleet
5. Drastic overexpansion by a major carrier
6. A series of major airline accidents
7. Surge of airline terrorism
8. Bankruptcy of a major airline
9. Computerization of reservations systems, making it possible for every passenger to minimize fare costs on their own personal computers
10. Creation of a futures market for airline tickets
11. Entrance of new large companies into the airline business
12. Establishment of several all-first-class airlines
13. A merger between a major airline and a bus company

14. A merger between two major airline carriers
15. Increasing domination by low-cost airlines
16. Penetration of U.S. markets by foreign air carriers
17. Purchase of airlines by travel or financing companies
18. Use of two-way cable television for ticket purchase and receipt of travel information within the home
19. Nationalization of airlines
20. Declaration that a major type of aircraft is unsafe

They similarly brainstormed possible government actions over the next two decades, listing "heavy control by local governments," "new safety regulations," and "government bailouts of failing airlines" among the thirty or so items in this category. After lunch, they covered categories that included technology (e.g., high-speed rail transportation between cities, automation to reduce human labor, a short-takeoff and -landing aircraft); economic developments (e.g., major oil supply disruption, rapid inflation); customers (e.g., reduced need to travel, increased use of private aircraft); and others relating to human resources, capital markets, international developments, and other arenas. By 3:00 P.M., they had identified over 200 major developments of this kind. A vote was conducted to choose the most significant events.

When the tabulation was complete, it was obvious that only a dozen events had attracted most of the votes, indicating clearly that these developments would require particular attention in the positioning decision. They examined each of them and reformulated them carefully, so that everybody agreed on what each one meant. For example, four of the events—originally listed as efficiency breakthrough, airline bankruptcy, decreased business travel and reregulation—were framed more clearly as follows:

1. Efficiency breakthrough. Technological developments reduce human labor in airline operations to at least 25 percent below current levels.
2. Airline bankruptcy. One or more of the currently major airlines files for bankruptcy.
3. Decreased business travel. The volume of business travel by airlines fails to increase because of greatly expanded use of teleconferencing and other advanced computer and communications technologies.
4. Reregulation. The deregulation of the airline industry is reversed, and the industry is reregulated to improve its economic viability or safety.

With all twelve events defined, Poulson asked each participant to write down his or her estimate of the probability of their occurring by the year 2020. When the estimates were tabulated, they showed a fairly strong consensus about the probability of some of the events but disagreement on others. He focused attention on the latter, asking those at the high or low ends of the distribution to present their rationales. Another round of probability estimates was conducted, and there began to be some convergence. Poulson pointed out that it wasn't necessary to force consensus but only to understand the reasons for disagreement. Since all the events on the short list had previously been judged to have a high impact on Global Airways, those that also had a high probability of occurrence seemed to demand immediate attention for positioning decisions. The other events, with lower probabilities of occurrence, required at least systematic monitoring and constant reevaluation over time.

By now it was late in the day, but there was one additional task to be performed. Poulson introduced the idea of a "cross-impact matrix," using the simple design shown in Figure 5. This could be used to provide a model of how each participant thinks the world works. He passed out a blank matrix containing all twelve events on the left-hand side and across the top and including five of the major indicators of performance. Poulson then asked each person to fill out the matrix.

At first, some of Global's veterans demurred; the task seemed too complicated. Once they started, however, they found that it was really quite challenging to try to understand how these important developments affect one another. Within thirty or forty minutes, all the participants had filled out their matrices. Poulson thanked them for their participation and asked for any reactions they might have to the day's experience. One said, "It gave me a chance to test my assumptions against those of the rest of

Fig. 5.　Cross-impact matrix.

Events	Probability of occurrence by year 2000	Events				Trends		
		1. Efficiency breakthrough	2. Airline bankruptcy	3. Decreased business travel	4. Regulation	Profitability of Global Airways	Quality of employee relationships	
1. Efficiency breakthrough	.8	■						
2. Airline bankruptcy	.9		■					
3. Decreased business travel	.3		+2	■				
4. Regulation	.4				■			

• To fill out this matrix, place a code in each cell representing the extent to which the occurrence of an event affects the probability of occurrence of another or the projection of a trend. A simple coding mechanism may be used, ranging from +3 (representing a greatly increased probability of occurrence) to zero (representing no impact) to −3 (representing a greatly diminished probability of occurrence). Blackened spaces are ignored. For example, the entry in cell 3-2 means that if business travel decreases, there is an enhanced probability of an airline bankruptcy.

the guys." Another remarked, "We've generated a lot of stuff and I'm impressed with how complex our competitive environment is becoming, but I'll be damned if I see how it all comes together." To this, Poulson replied, "I guess it's in my hands now. I'm going to take everything you've generated, including the cross-impact charts, and try to develop some themes around which we can organize the next meeting. I'll send you the report as soon as it is ready, and when you get it, I hope you'll spend a few minutes thinking about some of the strategic implications of these environments for Global Airways." The president closed the meeting by thanking everybody for their participation, enthusiasm and creativity. He adjourned the meeting, but nearly everybody stayed around in the hotel bar for several hours discussing the exercise.

The following day, Poulson began to write his report of the meeting. He first noticed that the group might have defined the scope of the inquiry too narrowly, since by limiting the discussion only to the movement of passengers and freight, they did not consider complementary or competing businesses such as hotels, restaurants and travel services that might offer profitable opportunities. He thought he'd better point that out in the report so it could be discussed at the next meeting. Examining the stakeholders' concerns and performance measures, he noticed that the performance measures only partially reflected the concerns of the major stakeholders and made a note that this too might require some additional attention. He then looked at the set of events identified by the participants, particularly those that had not made the top dozen in terms of significance. He thought many of those that had received lesser votes were interesting and made a note to include them in the scenarios.

With the help of one of his staff members, Poulson combined all fifteen cross-impact matrices into a single matrix. As expected, some of the cells of the combined matrix showed very strong consensus on the extent to which the events were interrelated, but others showed no consensus at all. He marked these cells for later examination. Then he looked at all twelve rows of the matrix. Some had many entries in them, showing that those events were significant driving forces; that is, their occurrence greatly changed the probability of occurrence of other events. These began to suggest themes for the scenarios. He looked down the columns and noticed that some columns had many entries in them, indicating that they were important reactor events—that is, that they were heavily driven by other developments. In these cases, he noted that an event may itself have a low probability of occurrence, but if certain other events occur, its probability may greatly increase, and these relationships were important to highlight. He also studied the combined matrix to try to understand which of the events tended to exert the greatest influence on the indicator trends that reflected the long-term performance of Global Airways.

Poulson then began to work on the scenarios. He wanted to write three or four little "stories," each of which combined sets of events and trends into a logical and consistent description of how the external environments of Global Airways might evolve in the next two decades. After studying the cross-impact matrix and the list of events, he began to see some patterns. Some of the events represented only minor changes from the current situation. These he clustered into a scenario labeled "business as usual," which showed how the environment could evolve with relatively little change from the current situation. Other events seemed to suggest more radical futures. Eventually, he clustered them into three other scenarios, which he labeled "market-driven," "government-driven," and "high economic pressure." The market-driven scenario was a generally optimistic one, permitting considerable expansion of the travel and airline industry. The high-economic-pressure scenario was one of generally worsening economic conditions. The government-driven scenario was characterized by much more government intervention in the industry than would be the case if the current trends continued. Each of the scenarios was designed to be distinctly different from the others, internally consistent, plausible, sufficiently detailed to be used for positioning decisions, and, most important, reflective of the expectations of the participants as expressed at the meeting.

Poulson included all of this material in the report and added as appendices all the lists that had been developed. The report was distributed to the participants ten days before the second meeting so that each person would have an opportunity to consider its strategic implications.

The participants met again, this time in the corporation's board room. Poulson began by asking for comments on the report and for any new insights the participants might have had since the prior meeting. After the general discussion, he asked the group to examine each scenario in turn and to list the strengths and weaknesses of the organization in dealing with each particular environment. The strengths tended to focus on the airline's management, image in the marketplace, route structure, and relative technological sophistication. The weaknesses tended to focus on problems with the union, difficulties in obtaining financing, and competitive weaknesses relative to some of the newer airlines.

Poulson turned to the major purpose of the second meeting, which was to identify positioning options using the categories developed earlier in this chapter. When he called for "reactive" positioning options, there were many suggestions, including:

- Developing a trend-monitoring system to provide early warning of environmental change
- Finding additional suppliers of aviation fuel to reduce dependence on current vendors
- Selling some older aircraft and leasing them back to reduce vulnerability in the event of major technological changes in aircraft design

Under "change the internal environment," the group listed a great variety of options, including the following:

- Changing the route structure
- Reconfiguring the aircraft fleet to increase the number of seats available
- Changing the organization structure to be more marketing-oriented, with special departments focused on particular market segments

Under the heading "change the external environment," the group identified options such as the following:

- Increasing lobbying efforts to get preferential treatment for airlines in the event of oil shortages
- Developing a new advertising program to make international travel more attractive to retired people
- Designing a method for direct sale of airline tickets to frequent users on their home computers

Finally, in the category labeled "establishing new relationships between the internal and external environments," many ideas were proposed, including the following:

- Developing a new arrangement with the union in which a portion of every salary includes a bonus that is paid only if the airline is profitable
- Acquiring a chain of travel agencies
- Seeking a joint agreement with a foreign government for the management of their national airlines

In a few hours, the group had identified more than 150 such positioning options. A few provoked laughter because they seemed so "way out," but even these usually stimulated the presentation of other serious proposals that all agreed were creative and innovative. When they were done, Poulson asked the group to vote on their ten top choices, those options that appeared to offer the greatest long-term payoff for Global Airways. After lunch, when the vote totals were revealed, it was obvious that four of the options had attracted far more attention than the rest. At this point, the president suggested that task forces be established to analyze each of the four major options and report back to the group in several months.

As there was still some time left, Poulson suggested that the remainder of the day be used to provide guidance to the task forces. The group addressed each option in turn, discussing various alternatives, the possible risks and rewards involved, resource requirements, and impacts upon various stakeholders. The task force chairmen had the opportunity to seek clarification from the entire group, so that they would be able to proceed with the analysis.

The president adjourned the session with a few remarks. He said:

I think we can be proud of the work we have done in these two meetings. I sense that we all share a common understanding of the possible directions of our future, and I'm impressed by how we seem to agree on the major strategies that are worth considering. I know that I was able to gain some new insight into issues that previously had appeared somewhat vague. I think we all benefited from trying to understand each other's views about what's going on and what could happen. Now we need to move ahead. I can promise you that we will give the most serious consideration to your task-force reports. If we can continue to work together like this, and I'm sure we will, I see a great future for this company. Thank you all for your help and I look forward to your reports.

Later that evening, as he reflected on the events of the day, the president felt he had made significant progress in earning the trust and commitment of his management colleagues. Because of the improvement in their common understanding of the external environment, he felt sure they would become more effective in managing functional areas. He also thought that everyone had developed a new sense of commitment to the future of the organization and had learned a great deal about their common concerns about vulnerability to change. For some, this had been one of a very few opportunities to deal with the longer-term future, and he saw this as a growth experience for them. For others, he thought the exercise would create an appetite for a more detailed and thorough analysis of future environments. Certainly, the task forces would have to look more deeply into the longer-range implications of the options identified by the group, and they probably would want to test some of their views against outside sources as they did so.

LESSONS FOR LEADERSHIP

We are not arguing that a two-day exercise is all that is needed for a leader to build trust in an organization. Obviously, trust is built up over a long period of time in a multitude of circumstances. All the same, the QUEST exercise does illustrate many of the important elements that build trust. It provides a crucible in which a leader can demonstrate the personal and organizational qualities that engender trust, such as mutual respect, competency and integrity.

Harold Williams gets at this when he describes his first experiences as chairman of the SEC:

If there is anything I feel good about [at the Commission], it's the way I came through in terms of my own personal values and my personal self. If you believe in your course, you gotta stay with it in terms of course and timing. I think it's tough at times—when the press are all over you and you start hearing from Capitol Hill and you know that even some of your own staff are feeding the stories and the corporate community is up in arms, and there were several times when it was *all* going that way and it gets kind of heavy. . . . But if you believe you're right, and you've got your own integrity—and I think that's where it really ends up—I mean: "Do you believe in what you're doing?"—And if you believe it, you stay with it. I couldn't change course and still respect myself.

171

By way of conclusion, let's return to the two most significant aspects of the QUEST exercise and the pivots around which this chapter on the management of trust turns: vision and positioning. Consider the way, in particular, positioning and trust are woven into the most fundamental activities of leaders:

1: All leaders face the challenge of overcoming resistance to change. People will resist change if they don't understand its purpose, if it causes too much uncertainty or disruption or if they feel it will affect them or the organization adversely. Some leaders try to overcome this by the simple exercise of power and control, but resistance often stiffens when people feel change is being imposed arbitrarily. Effective leaders, including most of those in our panel, learned early in their careers that it was far better to secure voluntary commitment to changes through open communication, participation and mutual trust. One of our leaders, the conductor of a major symphony orchestra, told us:

> Here I think I can say that in the small island we call the Philharmonic, I realized the state of true *civiltà*—considerate civility among equals. I hope it was not an illusion. I never had to say one negative word. Even in delicate situations, I explained my views to the orchestra. I did not impose them. The right response, if forced, is not the same as the right response when it comes out of conviction.

2:   The positioning decision aims at building a new community of common interests, shared circumstances and mutual trust. In many cases, this community will exist entirely inside the organization, as in the Global Airways example. More and more, however, leaders are extending the sense of community outward to involve selected customers and suppliers in some of the most fundamental deliberations of the organization, such as product design and distribution decisions. In some cases, the community stretches even further to encompass a network of alliances, mergers and joint ventures as seen, for example, in the large trading companies of Japan and the so-called Wintel axis of Microsoft Windows and Intel Corporation.

Creating such communities of interest casts the leader in the role of politician. To broker the needs of the various parties and gain their commitment, leaders must be astute negotiators—open and sensitive to the needs of all constituencies, honest and trustworthy in all matters and yet protective of the interests of their own organizations. As John Gardner says, "Skill in the building and rebuilding of community is not just another of the innumerable requirements of contemporary leadership. It is one of the highest and most essential skills a leader can command."[1]

3:   The leader is responsible for the set of ethics or norms that govern the behavior of people in the organization. Leaders can establish a set of ethics in several ways. One is to demonstrate by their own behavior their commitment to the set of ethics that they are trying to institutionalize. Consider the J. M.

Smucker Company of Orrville, Ohio, which dominates the nation's markets for jams and jellies with nearly three times the market share of its closest competitors. Ever since the first Mr. Smucker actually signed every label to show he personally stood behind each product, all company leaders in successive generations of Smuckers have served as personal models of integrity, social responsibility and high ethical standards. For example, company policy is to fill every jar with a bit more than the customer pays for. The company refuses to advertise on television shows that exploit sex or violence. It was the first in its industry to put nutritional information on every label, and it pays for a full-time federal inspector at every plant, though not required to do so. No one in the company dares cut any corners.

Leaders set the moral tone by choosing carefully the people with whom they surround themselves, by communicating a sense of purpose for the organization, by reinforcing appropriate behaviors and by articulating these moral positions to external and internal constituencies.

In the end, trust, integrity and positioning are all different faces of a common property of leadership—the ability to integrate those who must act with that which must be done so that it all comes together as a single organism in harmony with itself and its niche in the environment.

STRATEGY IV: THE DEPLOYMENT OF SELF

We are all afraid—for our confidence, for the future, for the world. This is the nature of the human imagination. Yet every man, every civilization, has gone forward because of its engagement with what it has set itself to do. The personal commitment of a man to his skill, the intellectual commitment and the emotional commitment working together as one, has made the Ascent of Man.

Jacob Bronowski
The Ascent of Man, 1973

When we asked our ninety leaders about the personal qualities they needed to run their organizations, they never mentioned charisma, or dressing for success, or time management or any of the other glib formulas that pass for wisdom in the popular press. Instead, they talked about persistence and self-knowledge; about willingness to take risks and accept losses; about commitment, consistency and challenge. But, above all, they talked about learning.

Leaders are perpetual learners. Some are voracious readers, like Harry Truman, who, as a young boy, spent countless hours in the town library and is reported to have read every book in it—several thousand volumes, including encyclopedias. Many learn mainly from other people. This is the style of Don Gevirtz, former chairman and CEO of the Foothill Group, who surrounds himself with politicians and academics, and Sam Walton, founder of the giant Wal-Mart chain, who was legendary for spending a great deal of his time with customers. Nearly all leaders are highly proficient in learning from experience. Most were able to identify a small number of mentors and key experiences that powerfully shaped their philosophies, personalities, aspirations and operating styles. And all of them regard themselves as "stretching," "growing" and "breaking new ground."

Learning is the essential fuel for the leader, the source of high-octane energy that keeps up the momentum by continually sparking new understanding, new ideas and new challenges. It is absolutely indispensable under today's conditions of rapid change and complexity. Very simply, those who do not learn do not long survive as leaders.

But aren't we all learning all the time? What's so special about leaders? Our interviews provided the answer. Leaders have discovered not just how to learn but how to learn *in an organizational context.* They are able to concentrate on what matters most to the organization and to use the organization as a learning environment. The most successful leaders have done this by developing a set of skills that Donald Michael calls "the new competence," which he identifies as follows:

1. Acknowledging and sharing uncertainty
2. Embracing error
3. Responding to the future
4. Becoming interpersonally competent (e.g., listening, nurturing, coping with value conflicts, etc.)
5. Gaining self-knowledge[1]

These skills came up many times in our discussions. We were told how leaders acknowledge and share uncertainty in task-force settings with colleagues, how they use their mistakes as learning experiences, how they engage in goal-setting exercises to force reexamination of current assumptions and priorities, how they use their interpersonal skills to encourage others to join in the search for new ideas, and how they constantly enhance their understanding of their own limits and biases by testing their views against those of knowledgeable colleagues and outside experts.

So leaders become experts in a particular kind of learning—learning in an organizational context. But still more important, and the factor that really differentiates leadership learning from other types of learning, is the role of the leader in *organizational learning,* the management of the collective self.

THE LEARNING ORGANIZATION

When the U.S. Justice Department decided that the twenty-two Bell Operating Companies valued at over $125 billion would have to be divested in a period of two years, AT&T faced more than a massive restructuring. It had to change its fundamental character. It would no longer be a regulated and protected public utility. Somehow it had to metamorphose into a competitive, risk-oriented corporation. Not only the leaders and the management but everyone connected with AT&T, individually and collectively, had to learn how to operate in a new mode. Totally new jobs, relationships, operating practices, goals, values and strategies had to be learned. As leader, AT&T Chairman Charles L. Brown had to direct his company through this perilous transition.

While dramatic, the AT&T example is far from unique. Organizations are constantly changing. Sometimes, as in mergers or plant relocations, these changes can be rapid and wrenching. More often, changes occur less rapidly and piecemeal—a new product here, some layoffs there, a joint venture somewhere else. But whether fast or slow, on a large scale or piecemeal, organizations are constantly transforming themselves. They are always learning.

Organizational learning is the process by which an organization obtains and uses new knowledge, tools, behaviors, and values. It happens at all levels in the organization—among individuals and groups as well as systemwide. Individuals learn as part of their daily activities, particularly as they interact with each other and the outside world. Groups learn as their members cooperate to accomplish common goals. The entire system learns as it obtains feedback from the environment and anticipates further changes. At all levels, newly learned knowledge is translated into new goals, procedures, expectations, role structures, and measures of success.

Perhaps the clearest example of organizational learning is provided by an army. Individual members of a military unit come to it with different values, education, aptitudes, motivations, and beliefs. Each individual must acquire some basic survival skills and a minimum level of proficiency in several physical and mental activities. Groups of soldiers learn how to act as a coherent unit, with each individual performing optimally in his or her assigned role and supporting others in the unit so that the joint enterprise is successful. Mutual trust, shared values, good internal communications, effective judgment under pressure, and rapid team response to external change must all be learned by the group, usually through a series of team training exercises prior to combat situations and continuous debriefing, reappraisal and reinforcement during engagements. Beyond this, the entire army must learn how to cope with a wide range of possible combat situations that may involve many different opponents, threats, missions, geographical conditions, and lead times. This occurs through analysis and war-gaming exercises that influence what weapons will be acquired, how the army should be structured and what rules are necessary to increase its readiness to act in reaction to, or in anticipation of, actual military engagements.

Corporations are no different. AT&T had to learn at the individual, group and organizational levels how to cope with divestment. General Motors is trying to learn at every level how to compete with Toyota under new market conditions. Johnson & Johnson learned very quickly how to deal with an environmental crisis—the deaths of several people from cyanide that had been placed in capsules of Extra-Strength Tylenol. IBM is learning how to deal with the combined power of Microsoft and Intel in the personal computer business, even while those firms are transforming themselves to cope with the new age of the Internet. In all these cases and thousands more, organizational learning is the way the corporation increases its survival potential by increasing its readiness to cope with new changes and opportunities.

Some organizational learning occurs wherever a group of people is engaged in a common enterprise. In a major work sponsored by the Club of Rome, an important distinction was made between maintenance learning and innovative learning, as follows:

Maintenance learning is the acquisition of fixed outlooks, methods, and rules for dealing with known and recurring situations. It enhances our problem-solving ability for problems that are given. It is the type of learning designed to maintain an existing system or an established way of life. Maintenance learning is, and will continue to be, indispensable to the functioning and stability of every society. But for long-term survival, particularly in times of turbulence, change, or discontinuity, another type of learning is even more essential. It is the type of learning that can bring change, renewal, restructuring, and problem reformulation—and which we have called innovative learning.[2]

In many organizations today, maintenance learning has been well developed and carefully institutionalized. This is necessary but not sufficient. In maintenance learning, current performance is compared only with past performance, not with what might have been or what is yet to be. Corrective action is designed to deal with perceived weaknesses and failures, not to build on strengths and new opportunities. And the work structures reinforce this entire tendency to restrict learning to what is necessary to maintain an existing system.

Innovative learning is more difficult because it focuses on preparing organizations for action in new situations, requiring the anticipation of environments that have not yet appeared. There are no familiar contexts within which innovative learning can take place; indeed, the construction of new contexts is precisely one of its tasks. Innovative learning deals with *emerging* issues—issues that may be unique, so that there is no opportunity to learn by trial and error; issues for which solutions are not known; and issues whose very formulation may be a matter of controversy and doubt. Therefore, innovative learning has often been neglected, with the result that many organizations have serious problems in adapting to changes in their environment. Managers are usually well equipped to handle maintenance learning, but it is the leader's responsibility to ensure innovative learning.

INNOVATIVE LEARNING

Just as people learn in different ways, so too do organizations. Much depends on the specific organization's purpose, culture, environment, operating style, and ability to absorb change. Six especially powerful modes of organizational learning are discussed briefly below.

1: *Reinterpretation of history.* Every organization has its experiences and traditions, sometimes embodied in anecdotes or legends of past successes and failures. At Ford they still talk about the Model T and the Edsel; at Data General they recount with glee their brash early days when they went up against Digital Equipment Corporation in the minicomputer market. When we examine these experiences in the light of new and evolving environments, it is often possible to draw lessons about what works under different sets of circumstances.

At AT&T, there is a solid tradition of service and quality built up over more than a hundred years. Everyone in the company knows the corporate legends of brave Bell System linemen fighting raging floods and blizzards to repair downed telephone wires. But now the challenge to the leadership is to redefine their tradition of service and quality in terms of AT&T's new reality—strong, aggressive, global competitors; rapidly changing technologies such as cellular phones, satellite communications and the World Wide Web; computer-savvy customers; and the voracious market appetites of its own progeny, the regional Bell companies and their successors.

2: *Experimentation.* An organization can test hypotheses about the direction of change in its environment by conducting controlled experiments and studying the effects. Corporations do this frequently with market research. Public agencies do it by conducting hearings on proposed legislation to obtain feedback. James MacGregor Burns has written that "executives operate by feel and by feedback. They grope their way into the future, moving one step at a time, ready always to fall back as they encounter obstacles."[3]

One corporation that has institutionalized experimentation as an organizational learning mode is 3M. Although it is a giant company with annual sales in excess of $15 billion and some 87,000 employees, 3M thrives by operating as a collection of small units. Work is organized into small projects that focus on particular products or markets, and people with new ideas have lots of freedom to test them out—nearly as much as if they were running a new business on their own. Over the years, 3M has had a remarkable record of growth and new-product innovation using this approach.

Of course, any firm with a research budget—3M

spends more than a billion dollars a year on research—may claim that experimentation is its major method for developing new products. At 3M and other entrepreneurial companies, however, this approach plumbs much further into all aspects of marketing, organizational design, production and distribution, as the firm learns how to launch and then grow its businesses.

3: *Analogous organizations.* Organizations learn by observing the experiences of other similar organizations. Corporate leaders read trade publications, attend association meetings and discuss common industry problems with other leaders. For many years after World War II, Japanese businessmen learned how to compete in world markets by studying analogous organizations overseas. Hordes of Japanese managers and engineers descended on U.S. companies, took millions of snapshots of production processes, interviewed tens of thousands of their American counterparts and went home to adapt the best of what they had learned to their own firms. Now the reverse appears to be happening. U.S. firms are avidly studying Japanese management methods. A dramatic example is "Buick City," a $300 million effort by General Motors to emulate the successful Japanese auto plants that link their own production and assembly processes with those of major suppliers in order to reduce inventory and improve quality.

AT&T realized that to be competitive after divestiture, it needed to become much more effective at marketing. It studied marketing processes in other electronic firms; hired Archie J. McGill, a top marketing executive, away from IBM; reorganized, like its competitors, into lines of business headed by leaders with full product authority; and established marketing agreements with high-powered retailers like Sears, Roebuck and Co. Wall Street still isn't sure AT&T has learned enough about marketing, but the changes have been rapid and affect every level of the company.

4: *Analytical processes.* Many organizations learn by a conscious process of analyzing trends in the external environment, identifying emerging issues, and designing new ways to cope with those issues. As Alfred P. Sloan, Jr., the legendary leader of General Motors, said, "The final act of business judgment is, of course, intuitive. . . . But the big work behind business judgment is in finding and acknowledging the facts and circumstances concerning technology, the market, and the like in their continually changing forms."[4] This theme kept recurring in our discussions with the ninety CEOs; intuitive judgment by the leader is essential, but it is effective only if it has been preceded by thorough analysis.

Often, learning is facilitated by models of change in the external environment that can be shared widely in the organization. A common type of model is the blueprint, depicting a proposed design of a facility, product, or piece of equipment. By studying the blueprint, individuals and groups in the organization develop a shared view of the proposed design and are able to explore its strengths, weaknesses and suitability. On a more conceptual level, "think pieces" describing proposed marketing plans or financial strategies serve as models of change in the same way. Analysis can include large linear programming models, econometric models and financial spread-sheet models that permit people to ask "what if?" questions. The only reason for building a complex systems model is to use it as an instrument for individual and organizational learning about the system it represents.

Listen to W. Brooke Tunstall, AT&T's director of corporate planning, describe some of the analytical background needed to restructure his firm:

> At AT&T Operational Headquarters in Basking Ridge, New Jersey, a remote 20×32 foot room serves as the status control center for the staggering job of disaggregating the Bell System. . . . The walls of this Corporate Divestiture Management Center are adorned with timeline charts, schedules, and graphic representations of critical issues. A computer terminal in one corner instantly displays any one of the 300 corporate assumptions, 2000 work activities, and/or 150 major events underlying divestiture planning.[5]

5: *Training and education.* Many organizations place a considerable emphasis on formal training processes. In fact, training and development is itself a major industry in the United States, rivaling in size the total spent by all colleges and universities on more traditional higher education. Motorola, for example, spends some $100 million a year on training and not for altruistic reasons—it expects to generate three dollars in sales for each training dollar. Every one of the more than 100,000 employees of

Motorola worldwide spends at least forty hours a year in these training programs. The company attributes much of its success in quality, new product development and manufacturing improvement to this effort.

Intel spends $3,000 per worker per year for management development activities. The giant consulting firm Arthur Anderson insists that every consultant take *at least* 130 hours annually for training. Jack Welch commits about 4 percent of GE's payroll for Crotonville and other developmental ventures. Perot Systems Chairman Mort Meyerson has established what he calls an "Intellectual Fitness Center" where novel and innovative ideas are auditioned.

Guess what? All of the above claim that their success is at least partly due to their developmental and training activities.

While much of this training is intended to improve individual skills, an increasing proportion is devoted to team building and group learning experiences. Some training programs—as, for example, courses on new technologies and industry trends—are clearly and directly related to helping the organization learn about changes in the environment. Beyond the formal courses, however, much informal training takes place as a by-product of committees and task forces set up for other purposes and in briefings by vendors, consultants and external auditors. These learning opportunities are often supplemented or amplified through formal communications channels such as newsletters and bulletin boards.

6: *Unlearning.* Often overlooked is the "unlearning" or discarding of old knowledge when actions by the organization clash with changed reality in the external environment. Problems such as the loss of a key customer often lead an organization to question its basic assumptions and to recombine or reorder them. A learning organization places a high value on these experiences because they supply a reality test and permit adjustments without which larger mistakes might be made in the future. For example, when Alfred P. Sloan, Jr., became the head of General Motors, he led that company through an unlearning process in which an entire system of management characterized by individual fiefdoms was discarded and a new system based on Sloan's design of decentralized but coordinated management was substituted.

More recently, a massive process of unlearning is taking place at Digital Equipment Corporation (DEC). Fundamental beliefs and operating practices that had developed over many years as a successful minicomputer manufacturer are being overthrown to get ready for the twenty-first century. To illustrate, it is moving from

- A company that often analyzed projects and deliberated for months before making commitments to one that is fast-moving and experimental. With only a slight exaggeration, the new way is "to propose something in the morning, implement in the afternoon and evaluate by the evening."[6]

- A company that depended almost entirely on its own proprietary technologies to one with many strategic alliances, some with firms that had been bitter rivals, like Microsoft and Oracle.
- A company culture based on exclusive promotion from within, stability of organizational structures and pride in service and technical excellence to one of increased recruitment of outsiders, changing organizational structures and a high value on risk taking. The old culture is being unlearned slowly and will eventually be forgotten by all but the "old-timers."

No one knows how successful DEC will be in unlearning its deeply rooted experiences and values, but nothing less than the future viability of the company may depend on it.

These six modes of innovative learning illustrate some of the ways organizations learn how to reconfigure themselves, replace old rules, improve their information flows, and revitalize their creative abilities. With effective organizational learning, judgment improves over time, conventional assumptions are continually being challenged and deeper levels of understanding of both the environment and the organization's role in it are constantly being achieved. But just as some kids are slow learners while others speed ahead, so too are some organizations more effective than others at innovative learning. The difference is leadership, without which organizational learning is unfocused—lacking in energy, force, cohesion and purpose.

LEADING THE LEARNING ORGANIZATION

We said that most of our ninety leaders were very much aware of the importance of their own learning abilities and needs. They were enthusiastic learners, open to new experiences, seeking new challenges and treating mistakes as opportunities for self-improvement. Fewer of them were equally conscious of their roles in organizational learning, but we did find evidence to suggest that much of their behavior served to direct and energize innovative learning. For example, when we talked to William Kieschnick, former president of ARCO, he told us:

> Early in my career I was working for several leaders in this company who were important role models. . . . They took risks on exploratory wells and since it was an uncertain situation, they tolerated dissent and other ideas from one another before they hammered out a course of action. . . . Ideas were important and creative tension was accepted as a working tool, and these things meant a lot in shaping my young life and my values.

Thus, William Kieschnick described how leaders stimulate learning by serving as role models. He was influenced to become a risk taker, and so were other promising young executives at the time. As a result, risk taking became a part of the ARCO culture, shaping goals, decision rules and the way the company did business. Later in his career, Kieschnick moved from heading a line organization to vice president for planning before becoming president. As a learner par excellence himself, Kieschnick was able to infuse the organization with his zeal for finding innovative new ways to operate in the oil business.

This quality of fostering organizational learning by example may be one of the most important functions of leadership. James MacGregor Burns points out that "the most marked characteristic of self-actualizers as potential leaders goes beyond Maslow's self-actualization; it is their capacity to learn from others and the environment—the capacity to be taught."[7] If the leader is seen as an effective learner from the environment, others will emulate that model, much as a child emulates a parent or a student emulates a teacher. The leader and the organization nurture each other, guiding the process of creative self-discovery by which each learns how to be most effective in a complex and changing environment.

As an example, consider what happened in 1992 when C. Michael Armstrong left a thirty-one-year career at IBM to become CEO of Hughes Aircraft Company. He freely admitted he had a lot to learn about the defense business. The organization helped him learn through a series of meetings with customers, executives and experts about their technologies, markets and possibilities. He spent weeks touring Hughes plant sites because, as he said, "I learn a lot. It's important to get that synergy between leadership and the organization, particularly in the midst of change."[8]

In turn, Armstrong helped the company learn how

to become more customer oriented, largely by his own example, through the people he promoted, his comments to the press and his choice of advertising messages. Together they began to learn how to reposition Hughes into new product/customer niches such as satellite distribution of entertainment programs. Within a few years, Hughes was transformed into a more viable competitor, far less dependent on aerospace, and well on its way to becoming a communications and electronics powerhouse.

Leaders can energize learning behavior by rewarding it when it happens. The leader can use the full range of rewards and punishments for this purpose, including compensation, recognition, control over allocation of resources, promotion to increased responsibilities, coveted assignments, expense accounts, freedom from routine and more.

What are some of the behaviors to be rewarded? First, the leader must reinforce long-range thinking, innovation and creativity. Speculation and anticipation of future developments should be legitimized and respected as an organizational activity. Change and experimentation must be embraced, as well as competition of ideas and the creation of new options. A general drive toward excellence and a shared commitment to the organization's missions must likewise be rewarded. New values and organizational arrangements should be encouraged to facilitate the sharing of knowledge and the identification of lower-level purposes with overall organizational missions.

For example, Citicorp is widely regarded as one of

the most innovative banks in the world. It pioneered the negotiable certificate of deposit, was early and aggressive in using automated teller machines, issued more bank credit cards than anyone else and is the world's largest private foreign lender. Walter B. Wriston, Citicorp's retired chairman and CEO, is widely regarded as having led the bank into this innovative mode. Consider the way he stimulated innovative learning:

- He authorized many experiments; almost any good idea that someone had was supported. Furthermore, he convinced managers that this was the way to succeed. As Richard S. Braddock, a Citicorp executive vice president, told the *Wall Street Journal*, "Having a lot of activity going on, and learning from it, is the best we can do."[9]
- He encouraged the hiring of bright nonconventional types like his successor, John Reed, an engineer who headed consumer banking, and Edwin P. Hoffman, an executive vice president with a Ph.D. in molecular biophysics. He promoted them quickly, too, when they succeeded. Many top managers at Citicorp are still in their thirties and early forties.
- He did not fire people when a risky venture failed. Instead, he'd assign the person to a more senior executive for a year or two to recover and recharge for another experiment. Consistent failure, of course, did result in dismissal, but Wriston seemed to think that if you

haven't ever made a mistake, you haven't been trying hard enough.

Other rewards for innovation are also possible. Jerry Neely, former CEO of Smith International, told us, "If a division manager tells us that they are going to be doing some R&D work in a certain area, we know that will impact their earnings so we will buy off on that concept and give the manager a lower return-on-investment target for several years."

Neely also gives young, adventuresome people considerable authority to make decisions. As he describes it: "We keep pushing more and more decisions on people, giving them larger expenditure limits and hiring limits, and more discretion in terms of the financial impact of their performance. . . . Out of the twelve division presidents, only two are over fifty years old and these divisions run from $30 million to $400 million in size."

There are many other ways that a leader can help stimulate organizational learning. Gil Friesen, former president of A&M Records, told us he builds a creative environment by hiring talented young people and nurturing their innovativeness. Many leaders have developed a decision style in which they refuse to approve a project unless the department proposing it can also offer a range of well-developed alternatives, thereby forcing a search for other options. Others use suggestion boxes and prizes to stimulate a search for new ideas, or they bring in consultants to run "focused group sessions" to stimulate group creativity. The possibilities are endless.

ORGANIZING FOR INNOVATIVE LEARNING

While the leader provides the stimulus and focus for innovative learning, some organizations, like some children, are learning-handicapped. They just seem to be so rigid and inflexible that nothing less than a major crisis can change them. That's the bad news. The good news is that leaders can redesign organizations to become more receptive to learning. They can do this by designing *open organizations* that are both *participative* and *anticipative*.

An open organization is one that is designed to have constant, intense interactions with its external environments and to respond quickly and flexibly to new information. In an open organization, people share a set of norms, values, and priorities that contribute to learning—alertness to change, a search for new challenges and options, and respect for innovation and risk taking. An open organization is also future-oriented, in the sense that much of its behavior is governed by anticipations of future threats and opportunities and a concern for the future consequences of current strategies. Much attention is paid to information and communication systems, the channels through which learning is shared by all parts of the organization. Units of manageable size are created, small enough to let employees feel genuine responsibility for the unit and to measure their progress in accommodating to environmental change.

Computer manufacturers and software firms are particularly good examples of flexible, open organizations. Internally, they are usually dominated by project and program structures that can easily be rearranged. There's considerable job mobility both within firms and between them, so lessons learned in one place are diffused quickly. A small army of sales and service personnel maintains close relationships with customers so that new needs are easily identified. Technical people attend frequent conferences to share the latest developments. Suppliers are involved early in the design of new products. User associations, securities analysts, and a vigorous trade press provide continuous critical feedback on the firm's decisions. Managers are chosen who can absorb all of this information and who are quick to form new programs and project teams to react to new situations. The entire industry has learned the importance of flexibility, and bankruptcy awaits those who are unable to cope with rapid change.

Participation is the second element in the design of a learning organization. As Franklin Murphy, former chairman of the Times-Mirror Publishing Company, told us, "people have a stake in an idea if they participated in its creation; then they'll work much harder, in a much more dedicated way, to bring it to success." In groups, individuals learn from each other what is happening in the outside world, what is worthy of attention, what achievements are possible and desirable, and how responsibilities should be apportioned. Through cooperative processes, they share their understanding and stimulate each other to invest time and energy for the organization's benefit.

Leaders recognize the importance of participation

to learning. At Olga Corporation, a rapidly growing apparel manufacturer, Chairman Jan Erteszek, says, "A business corporation is not only an economic entity but a community, possibly *the* central community of our times.... Creative meetings have been greatly responsible for our leadership in product innovation and quality."[10] What the leader hopes to do is to unite the people in the organization into a "responsible community," a group of interdependent individuals who take responsibility for the success of the organization and its long-term survival. In doing so, leaders contribute to the competence of individuals and groups to manage complexity in their environment.

Finally, anticipation must be designed into the learning organization. This usually occurs by establishing an effective planning process and rewarding people who use it as a mechanism for managing change. As Donald Michael said, "Planning is the mode by which a complex social organism can learn what it seeks to become, perceive how to attempt to do so, test whether progress has been made, and reevaluate along the way whether the original goal is still desirable."[11]

In its most general sense, planning is nothing more than a process of making informed judgments about the future and acting on them. However, it can be institutionalized in a formal planning mechanism through which the organization identifies and evaluates new issues, designs and considers alternative policies, generates a consensus about appropriate actions and provides legitimacy for major changes in direction. In a study by James Brian Quinn of nine large corporations, the most important contributions of formal planning processes were found to be the following:

1. They created a network of information that would not otherwise have been available.
2. They periodically forced operating managers to extend their time horizons and see their work in a larger framework.
3. They required vigorous communications about goals, strategic issues and resource allocations.
4. They systematically taught managers about the future so they could better intuitively calibrate their short-term or interim decisions.
5. They often created an attitude about and a comfort factor concerning the future; that is, managers felt less uncertain about the future and consequently were more willing to make commitments that extended beyond short time horizons.
6. They often stimulated longer-term special studies that could have high impact at key junctures for specific strategic decisions.[12]

To summarize, leaders can provide the proper setting for innovative learning by designing open organizations in which participation and anticipation work together to extend the time horizons of decision makers, broaden their perspectives, allow for the sharing of assumptions and values and facilitate the development and use of new approaches. By learning as much as possible about its changing environment and where it seems to be going, the organization can develop a sense of its purpose, direction and desired future state. When this sense is widely shared in the organization, the energies of all the members of the organization are aligned in a common direction and each individual knows how his or her own efforts contribute to the overall thrust. With an understanding of where the environment is going and where the organization is heading, it is much easier both to position the organization so as to take advantage of ongoing trends and to design an appropriate social architecture that supports the overall thrust.[13]

In all of this, the role of the leader is much like that of the conductor of an orchestra. The real work of the organization is done by the people in it, just as the music is produced only by the members of the orchestra. The leader, however, serves the crucial role of seeing that the right work gets done at the right time, that it flows together harmoniously, and that the overall performance has the proper pacing, coordination and desired impact on the outside world. The great leader, like the great orchestra conductor, calls forth the best that is in the organization. Each performance is a learning experience which enables the next undertaking to be that much more effective—more "right" for the time, place and instruments at hand. And if in the long run the organization succeeds, it doesn't at all detract from the quality of everyone else's work to suggest that it was the leader who made it possible for the organization to learn how to perfect its contribution.

TAKING CHARGE:
LEADERSHIP AND
EMPOWERMENT

But hard it is to learn the mind of any mortal, or the heart, till he be tried in chief authority. Power shows the man.

Sophocles, *Antigone*

Leaders have a significant role in creating the state of mind that is the society. They can serve as symbols of the moral unity of the society. They can express the values that hold the society together. Most important, they can conceive and articulate goals that lift people out of their petty preoccupations, carry them above the conflicts that tear a society apart, and unite them in the pursuit of objectives worthy of their best efforts.

John W. Gardner[1]

"The employees were willing to take a chance because they felt a part of something magic and they *wanted* to work that extra hour or make that extra call, or stay on that extra Saturday. Maybe if we had a different management that did exactly the same thing, except to instill that—yes, *magic*—we would not have made it." That was Jerry Neely talking about his company, Smith International, the world's second largest manufacturer of oil drilling and rigging equipment.

Werner Erhard, the founder of est, didn't use the word "magic," but he seemed to be talking about something parallel:

> . . . There is this place in people, where they are aligned, where they don't need to be told what to do; they more or less sort out for themselves what needs to be done and where they can work in harmony with other people, not as a function of a bunch of agreements or contracts, but out of a sense of harmony. . . . It's something akin to what you see on a sailboat in a crew working together when one of the lines breaks. Very few, if any, orders are given and nobody waits for the other guy and nobody gets in the other guy's way—there's something about sailors in which there is an alignment, a kind of coming from the whole and nobody needs to give orders.

What these two leaders refer to as either "magic" or "alignment" is the epiphany of effective leadership: leaders as catalysts, leaders capable of deploying their ideas and themselves into some consonance and thereby committing themselves to a greater risk—the exposure and intimacy that most of us emotionally yearn for, rhetorically defend, but in practice shun. At their best, these leaders—a fairly disparate group in many superficial ways—commit themselves to a common enterprise and are resilient enough to absorb the conflicts; brave enough, now and then, to be transformed by its accompanying energies; and capable of sustaining a vision that encompasses the whole organization. The organization finds its greatest expression in the consciousness of a common social responsibility, and that is to translate that vision into a living reality.

This is "transformative leadership,"[2] the province of those leaders we've been discussing throughout this book, leaders identical to John Gardner—and those he alludes to: leaders who can shape and elevate the motives and goals of followers. Transformative leadership achieves significant change that reflects the community of interests of both leaders and followers; indeed, it frees up and pools the collective energies in pursuit of a common goal.

Now we can make some sweeping generalizations about transformative leadership: It is collective, there is a symbiotic relationship between leaders and followers, and what makes it collective is the subtle interplay between the followers' needs and wants and the leader's capacity to understand, one way or another, these collective aspirations. Leadership is "causative," meaning that leadership can invent and create institutions that can empower employees to satisfy their needs. Leadership is morally purposeful and elevating, which means, if nothing else, that leaders can, through deploying their talents, choose purposes and visions that are based on the key values of the workforce and create the social architecture that supports them. Finally, leadership can move followers to higher degrees of consciousness, such as liberty, freedom, justice and self-actualization.

But as we've made plain in our introductory chapter and implied throughout the book, most organizations are managed, not led. Management typically consists of a set of contractual exchanges, "you do this job for that reward," or, as Erhard said, "a bunch of agreements or contracts." What gets exchanged is not trivial: jobs, security, money. The result, at best, is compliance; at worst, you get a spiteful obedience. The end result of the leadership we have advanced is completely different: it is empowerment. Not just higher profits and wages, which usually accompany empowerment, but an organizational culture that helps employees generate a sense of meaning in their work and a desire to challenge themselves to experience success. Leadership stands in the same relationship to empowerment that management does to compliance. The former encourages a "culture of pride," while the latter suffers from the "I only work here" syndrome. Our hope for this book and our readers is to extricate the reality of transformative leadership from that which is either accidental or mystical to something that is masterable, knowable and graspable and can be made available to all future and present leaders. Which inevitably leads us to the topic of management education.

MANAGEMENT EDUCATION

"Management education" is, unfortunately, the appropriate description for that which goes on in most formal educational and training programs, both within and outside universities. Management education relies heavily, if not exclusively, on mechanistic, pseudorational "theories" of management and produces tens of thousands of new MBAs each year. The gap between management education and the reality of leadership in the workplace is disturbing, to say the least, and probably explains why the public seems to hold such a distorted (and negative) image of American business life.

But the image problem, though serious, is hardly the major problem. The major problem is that what management education does do moderately well is to train good journeymen/women managers; that is, the graduates acquire technical skills for solving problems. They are highly skilled problem solvers and staff experts. Problem solving, while not a trivial exercise, is far removed from the creative and deeply human processes required of leadership. What's needed is not *management* education but *leadership* education.

The typical course that passes for management education starts with a number of dubious assumptions such as "If you don't know what your objectives are, try to identify them." Or "If you don't know what your alternatives are, search until you find them." Or "If you don't know what to do, then undertake research (or hire consultants) to establish the cause-and-effect connections in your activities."

Such recommendations are not altogether stupid. There's some experience we can cite where efforts to establish goals can be positive, but it's rarely of long-run help. The idea of establishing goals first and then taking action relies on a rationalistic fiction that has obvious limitations, such as: How does one go about searching for alternatives? What are the techniques of search? How do you go about finding alternatives that have not been invented? And how do you avoid the creation of pseudoalternatives as ways of making a preferred alternative look good?

The world is far more fascinatingly complex than the straight linear thinking that dominates so much of what passes for management education: the nature of the problem itself is often in question, the information (and its reliability) is problematical, there are multiple and conflicting interpretations and different value orientations, the goals are unclear and conflicting, and we could go on and on. The point is that most management education makes certain assumptions that are dangerously misleading—namely, that the goals are clear, alternatives known, technology and its consequences certain and perfect information available. It sounds terrifyingly similar to the courses in microeconomics on which, unfortunately, so much of management education is based.

What makes matters even worse is that much of the human element is either avoided or shortchanged in most curricula. To the best of our knowledge, the four basic competencies we've outlined in this book are honored more in the breach than in execution. And when the "human side" is touched on here or there—as it is in the elite schools of management—it is often accompanied by embarrassed sighs or academic pejoratives such as "soft" or "poetic" or "impressionistic"—attitudes and words that discredit the ideas before they're even understood.

DISPELLING MYTHS

It might be useful now to turn to some recurring myths that, in our view, both diminish much of what passes for management education and, at the same time, tend to discourage potential leaders from "taking charge" of their organizations. These myths include the following:

Myth 1: *Leadership is a rare skill.* Nothing can be further from the truth. While *great* leaders may be as rare as great runners, great actors or great painters, everyone has leadership potential, just as everyone has some ability at running, acting and painting. While there seems to be a dearth of great leaders today, particularly in high political offices, there are literally millions of leadership roles throughout the country and they are all filled, many of them more than adequately.

More important, people may be leaders in one organization and have quite ordinary roles in another. We know of a college professor who is a general in the U.S. Army Reserves and a clerk at JCPenney's who is a powerful leader of a church group. A taxi driver we know is the director of an amateur theater group, and a retired beer salesman is the mayor of a decent-sized town.

The truth is that leadership opportunities are plentiful and within the reach of most people.

Myth 2: Leaders are born, not made. Biographies of great leaders sometimes read as if they had entered the world with an extraordinary genetic endowment, that somehow their future leadership role was preordained. Don't believe it. The truth is that major capacities and competencies of leadership can be learned, and we are all educable, at least if the basic desire to learn is there and we do not suffer from serious learning disorders. Furthermore, whatever natural endowments we bring to the role of leadership, they *can* be enhanced; nurture is far more important than nature in determining who becomes a successful leader.

This is not to suggest that it is easy to learn to be a leader. There is no simple formula, no rigorous science, no cookbook that leads inexorably to successful leadership. Instead, it is a deeply human process, full of trial and error, victories and defeats, timing and happenstance, intuition and insight. Learning to be a leader is somewhat like learning to be a parent or a lover; your childhood and adolescence provide you with basic values and role models. Books can help you understand what's going on, but for those who are ready, most of the learning takes place during the experience itself. As one of our leaders put it concerning his own leadership development, "It's not easy, you know, learning how to lead; it's sort of like learning how to play the violin in public."

Myth 3: Leaders are charismatic. Some are, most

aren't. Among the ninety there were a few—but damned few—who probably correspond to our fantasies of some "divine inspiration," that "grace under stress" we associated with J.F.K. or the beguiling capacity to spellbind for which we remember a Churchill. Our leaders were all "too human"; they were short and tall, articulate and inarticulate, dressed for success and dressed for failure, and there was virtually nothing in terms of physical appearance, personality or style that set them apart from their followers. Our guess is that it operates in the other direction; that is, charisma is the result of effective leadership, not the other way around, and that those who are good at it are granted a certain amount of respect and even awe by their followers, which increases the bond of attraction between them.

Myth 4: *Leadership exists only at the top of an organization.* We may have played into this myth unintentionally by focusing exclusively on top leadership. But it's obviously false. In fact, the larger the organization, the more leadership roles it is likely to have. General Motors has thousands of leadership roles available to its employees. In fact, nowadays many large corporations are moving in the direction of creating more leadership roles through "intrapreneurship," the creation of small entrepreneurial units within the organization with the freedom and flexibility to operate virtually as small independent businesses. William Kieschnick, former CEO of ARCO, told us that one of the biggest problems he faced was to inspire the entire multibillion-dollar corporation "with an entrepreneurial spirit . . .

which means that we need leadership at every single unit, at every level—and I think this is happening." As organizations learn more about this, there will almost certainly be a multiplication of the leadership roles available to employees.

Myth 5: The leader controls, directs, prods, manipulates. This is perhaps the most damaging myth of all. As we have stressed with monotonous regularity, leadership is not so much the exercise of power itself as the empowerment of others. Leaders are able to translate intentions into reality by aligning the energies of the organization behind an attractive goal. It is Carlo Maria Giulini, formerly the conductor of the Los Angeles Philharmonic, who claims that "what matters most is human contact, that the great mystery of music making requires real friendship among those who work together." It is Irwin Federman, past president of Monolithic Memories, who believes that "the essence of leadership is the capacity to build and develop the self-esteem of the workers." It is William Hewitt, who took over John Deere and Company in the mid-fifties when it was a sleepy, old-line farm-implements firm and made it into a world leader because, as one employee put it, "Hewitt made us learn how good we were."

These leaders lead by pulling rather than by pushing; by inspiring rather than by ordering; by creating achievable, though challenging, expectations and rewarding progress toward them rather than by manipulating; by enabling people to use their own initiative and experiences rather than by denying or constraining their experiences and actions.

Myth 6: The leader's sole job is to increase share-holder value. Most executives, economists and investors applaud this statement. In our view, it is not so much wrong as misleading and too limited. Exclusive attention to shareholder value often leads to decisions that slight other important stakeholders at great cost to the long-term viability of the organization. For example, consider the typical downsizing scenario. A CEO slashes today's payroll to improve next year's bottom line for shareholders. Investors celebrate, but in the process worker morale and productivity often sink, customer service declines and product quality is jeopardized. We find that a pretty strange measure of effective leadership! At the very least, the statement needs to be revised to read, "an important part of the leader's job is to increase *long-term* shareholder value," but even that falls somewhat short.

In earlier chapters, we showed how leadership differed from management. Here's another distinction that grows out of our conversations with successful leaders. Leaders expect managers to *operate* the organization, paying attention almost exclusively to bottom-line performance. Though hardly uninterested in current performance, leaders see themselves as having a different responsibility. Their primary concern is in *building* the organization to ensure its long-term viability and success. The leader is the major instrument an organization has for articulating its dreams, pointing the way toward their achievement and helping people work together effectively to create brighter futures. For real leaders, then, making a profit is a *requirement*, not a vision or goal; nor does it animate or empower the workforce. The excessive and exclusive obsession with the enshrined "bottom line" will only lead to destructive "short-termism" along with a tremendous cost to the long-term viability of the organization. Thus a broader and, in our view, far more satisfactory statement of the leader's main role would be as follows: "The leader's primary responsibility is to serve as trustee and architect of the organization's future, building the foundations for its continued success."

Once these myths are cleared away, the question becomes not one of how to become a leader but rather how to improve one's effectiveness at leadership—how to "take charge" of the leadership in an organization. While these lessons from some of America's great leaders may help to refocus management education—as we hope it will—along the lines suggested here, it is equally important for organizations to modify their social architecture to encourage and develop the style of transformative leadership we have been advocating.

TOWARD THE NEW MILLENNIUM

To this point, we've been examining the lessons of our ninety leaders. We set out to distill the essence of what worked for them as they gained their experience and honed their skills over the past several decades. To mine this lode of information, we've been digging in the past, albeit the recent past. But what's next? What new demands are likely to be made upon leaders in the early part of the next century? Will leaders need new skills and values, and how might they begin to prepare for them?

Here we move to less solid ground, as we speculate on future trends and their implications. Let's start by assuming that leadership will continue to be concerned with marshaling the commitment, energies and resources of an organization to move it a particular direction. We expect that most of the time-tested personal characteristics identified in this book—vision, passion, integrity, self-knowledge, empowerment, doing things right—will continue to be important, but perhaps there'll be other factors as well.

The key driver in the twenty-first century is likely to be the speed and turbulence of technological change—a virtual tsunami of change. It makes the future tense. Already we feel the rumbles of a new round of technological eruptions in fields as diverse as genetics, communications, materials, oceanography, medicine, microminiaturization and entertainment. Technology explodes like nuclear fission, with every new breakthrough triggering others in an accelerating cascade of changes. The effects are pervasive. It's hard to think of any industry or government agency that won't find itself heavily dependent on technology in their operations, products or services.

The implications for leaders could be profound. Increasingly, they'll have to place high-stakes bets on emerging technologies whose benefits and consequences can be only partly understood in advance, and with considerable uncertainty. But that's just the beginning. As Will Rogers said, "It isn't enough to be on the right track. If you aren't moving, you can still get hit by a train."

New technologies begin to grow old the day they're installed. They need constant care and feeding, development and improvement until the day of reckoning, when a new batch comes on-line. Thus, nurturing technological change and facilitating transitions from one generation of product and process technologies to another is likely to become a major challenge and potential cost trap for twenty-first-century leaders.

Bill Gates at Microsoft and Andrew Grove at Intel may only be the leading edge of a new generation of technologically savvy leaders who feel comfortable making these kinds of decisions. Certainly, few leaders will be able to survive without being able to create and sustain organizational cultures in which new technologies are embraced and implemented quickly —time after time. They may well find themselves repeating this prayer from an African-American church: "Lord, we're not what we want to be, we're not what we need to be, we're not what we are going to be, but thank God Almighty, we're not what we used to be."[3]

As Peter Drucker and others have been predicting for some time, most organizations will be filled with knowledge workers. They'll have substantial expertise in their own areas, often beyond that of their so-called leaders, and they'll expect to be free to make decisions in their own areas of competence. They'll exercise considerable influence over their own work and often set their own schedules. Many of them will be leaders themselves, heading project teams or programs, so top executives will have to become what our colleague James O'Toole calls "leaders of leaders."[4] In such a setting, decisions are shaped far less by leadership authority than by collaboration, shared values and mutual respect.

As the half-life of new knowledge decreases, workers may feel they're constantly being bombarded by changes. Along with added responsibility to act on the organization's behalf, they'll have fewer middle management buffers to insulate them from the turbulence they experience daily both at work and at home—and fewer safety nets to protect them against the consequences of their mistakes and those of others. All this will make their organizational lives interesting, but also confusing, uncertain, risky and stressful.

Therefore, the challenge to leaders will be to act as compassionate coaches, dedicated to reducing stress by ensuring that the whole team has everything it needs—from human and financial resources to emotional support and encouragement—to work together effectively and at peak performance most of the time. Recognizing, developing and celebrating the distinctive skills of each individual will become critically important to organizational survival. In the new global, multicultural workplace where employees have different languages, values and loyalties, this may well challenge leaders to new heights of interpersonal sensitivity, understanding and commitment to the best that human diversity has to offer.

Some of the technological changes, especially in computers and communications, could shatter traditional organizational designs. Already we appear to be entering a centrifugal age that is spinning power and decision making out to the perimeters of organizations, wherever in the world an employee "interfaces" with a customer, supplier or joint-venture partner. Activities are being distributed over space and time, with work going on not just around the clock but around the globe. Increasingly, transactions occur in cyberspace, with information transmitted instantly and simultaneously to all who need to know. Organizations are becoming flatter, less hierarchical and more intricately networked than ever before.

With these forces at work, people's energies, actions and ambitions would fly off in every direction without a shared vision to provide a field that can align the many disparate and distributed tasks and units. It will no longer be enough for leaders to issue pious platitudes about innovation while they eviscerate their research departments. Slogans of the week just won't cut it. Leaders will have to be architects and cheerleaders for change—true visionaries who are able to point to destinations that are so desirable and credible that workers will enthusiastically sign on to become partners in making it happen. Though this will be much tougher amid the technologically driven turbulence of the next few decades, it is likely to become the indispensable litmus test of twenty-first-century leadership.

Today, leaders are prized for their ability to downsize, stream me and turn around organizations that have grown bloated and unwieldy. Tomorrow, they will be expected to create totally new organizational forms that position their enterprises in anticipation of future changes. They'll preside over endless experiments to discover ways to deliver new benefits or services to clients who may not even know they need them yet. Since no organization can possibly be all things to all people, the leader will be constantly challenged to forge major alliances and partnerships with others to achieve mutual goals. Thus the role of leader as social architect will be expanded, and skills such as negotiation, technology assessment and design of organizational cultures could grow in importance for aspiring leaders.

All these changes, as summarized in Table 3, will create a need for millions of new leaders in the future. In the end, the leaders who succeed best will be those who are best able to (1) set direction during turbulent times; (2) manage change while still providing exceptional customer service and quality; (3) attract resources and forge new alliances to accommodate new constituencies; (4) harness diversity on a global scale; (5) inspire a sense of optimism, enthusiasm and commitment among their followers; and (6) be a leader of leaders, especially regarding knowledge workers. Leadership in the twenty-first century is not a job for wimps; but then, it never was.

Table 3   Likely Model of Twenty-First-Century Leadership

From	To ...
Few leaders, mainly at the top; many managers	Leaders at every level; fewer managers
Leading by goal-setting; e.g., near-term profits, ROI	Leading by vision—creating new directions for long-term business growth
Downsizing, benchmarking for low cost, high quality	Also creating domains of uniqueness, distinctive competencies
Reactive/adaptive to change	Anticipative/futures-creative
Designer of hierarchical organizations	Designer of flatter, distributed, more collegial organizations; leader as social architect
Directing and supervising individuals	Empowering and inspiring individuals, but also facilitating teamwork
Information held by few decision makers	Information shared with many, both internally and with outside partners
Leader as boss, controlling processes and behaviors	Leader as coach, creating learning organizations
Leader as stabilizer, balancing conflicting demands and maintaining the culture	Leader as change agent, creating agenda for change, balancing risks and evolving the culture and the technology base
Leader responsible for developing good managers	Leader also responsible for developing future leaders; serving as leader of leaders

A FINAL NOTE

What Tolstoy said about families—that "all happy families resemble each other while each unhappy family is unhappy in its own way"—turns out to be true about leaders too. Our ninety leaders *do* resemble each other. They all have the ability to translate intention into reality and to sustain it. They all make a sharp distinction between leadership and management by concerning themselves with the organization's basic purposes, why it exists, its general direction and value system. They are all able to induce clarity regarding their organization's vision. (As a vice president and number-two man to one of our CEOs put it, "The thing about Joe [his CEO] is that even when his advice to us turns out to be wrong, it's always *clear*.") They are all able to arouse a sense of excitement about the significance of the organization's contribution to society.

These distinctions between leaders and managers have always existed, but they take on greater importance in the contemporary context. That's because nothing is more central to modern organizations than their capacity to cope with complexity, ambiguity, uncertainty—in short, with spastic change. And in an era of rapid change, it becomes necessary for the organization to be more future-oriented, more concerned with selecting the proper *direction* (or as the former president of Swarthmore College, Theodore Friend III, put it: "the angle into the wind"). This makes leadership all the more necessary today compared with more stable times, when

the relationship between organizations and the environment was better understood, when there weren't
too many games of Chinese baseball around, when
even managers may have been effective.

We fervently wish that there were available to us a
simple way to discuss, let alone teach, leadership in
a more straightforward, step-by-step way. But that
would be misleading and, in the end, not at all help-
ful. We're reminded of a story told about Lee
Strasberg, the famous acting teacher. He was directing two acting students in a love scene and he asked
the young woman what she was thinking of to evoke
the required emotion. She said something like,
". . . you know . . . spring . . . longing for and loving
him . . . you know." Strasberg then asked her if she'd
ever made fruit salad and she said that she had, and
he asked her how she made it. She asked him if he
was serious, did he really want her to tell how she
made fruit salad in front of everybody . . . "here in
class?" He assured her that he did.

"OK," she said, "I take an apple and I peel it and I
cut it into pieces. And I take a banana and I peel it
and cut it into slices. Then I peel an orange and cut
it into slices. Maybe I take a few cherries and pit
them and cut them into slices. And then I mix it all
together."

Then Strasberg said: "That's right, that's how you
make fruit salad. And until you pick up each piece of
fruit, one at a time, peel it, and cut it into slices, you
don't have fruit salad. You can run over the fruit with
a steam roller, but you won't have fruit salad. Or you
can sit in front of the fruit all night, saying, 'OK, fruit

salad!' Nothing will happen, though, until you pick up each piece and peel it and cut it up."[5]

But acting, even creating the emotion of love, is a cinch compared with leadership. While we can elucidate as clearly as possible the principles we've been able to learn from our effective leaders, the process of internalizing them is a lifetime challenge. In two other books, one of the authors explores this theme further, showing the path that twenty-eight outstanding leaders followed as they invented themselves and their careers during their lifetimes and using their lessons as the basis for a workbook to help readers examine their own progress in internalizing the principles of leadership.[6]

We began this book by saying that our present crisis calls out for leadership at every level of society and in all organizations that compose it. Without leadership of the kind we've been calling for, it is hard to see how we can shape a more desirable future for this nation or the world. The absence or ineffectiveness of leadership implies the absence of vision, a dreamless society, and this will result, at best, in the maintenance of the status quo or, at worst, in the disintegration of our society because of lack of purpose and cohesion.

We must raise the search for new leadership to a national priority. We desperately need women and men who can take charge, and we hope that you, the reader, will be among them. What can be more consequential and inspiriting?

NOTES

Mistaking Charge

1. For more on "transformative leadership," see Warren Bennis, "The Artform of Leadership," in S. Srivastva, ed., *The Executive Mind* (San Francisco: Jossey-Bass, 1983), chap. 1. The phrases "transformative leadership" and "transactional leadership" come from James MacGregor Burns's seminal book *Leadership* (New York: Harper & Row, 1978), chaps. 3 and 4.
2. Daniel Yankelovich & Associates, *Work and Human Values* (New York: Public Agenda Foundation, 1983), pp. 6–7.
3. John Naisbitt, *Megatrends* (New York: Warner, 1982).
4. Douglas McGregor, *The Human Side of Enterprise* (New York: McGraw-Hill, 1960).
5. Robert Townsend, *Up the Organization* (New York: Fawcett, 1970).
6. Philip E. Slater, *The Pursuit of Loneliness* (Boston: Beacon, 1970).
7. Jonas Salk, *Man Unfolding* (New York: Harper & Row, 1972).
8. Ilya Prigogine, *Order Out of Chaos* (New York: Bantam, 1984).
9. Tom Peters, *Thriving on Chaos* (New York: Knopf, 1987).

10. Peter F. Drucker, *The New Realities* (New York: Harper & Row, 1989).
11. Charles Handy, *The Age of Paradox* (Boston: Harvard Business School Press, 1994).
12. Rosabeth Moss Kanter, *The Change Masters* (New York: Simon & Schuster, 1983).
13. Burns, op. cit.

Leading Others, Managing Yourself

1. *Profile of a Chief Executive Officer* (New York: Heidrick & Struggles, 1982).
2. George Bernard Shaw, *Man and Superman* (Baltimore: Penguin, 1973), p. 84.
3. Alfred P. Sloan, Jr., *My Years with General Motors* (New York: Doubleday, 1946; Anchor, 1972), p. 65.
4. Don Marquis, *The Lesson of the Moth* (New York: Pushcart Press, 1976), pp. 167–68.
5. Albert Bandura, "Self-efficacy Mechanism in Human Agency," *American Psychologist*, February 1982, pp. 122–47.

Strategy I: Attention Through Vision

1. David Halberstam, *The Powers That Be* (New York: Dell, 1979), p. 40.
2. Jonathan Carr, "Success as a State of Mind," *Financial Times*, Feb. 13, 1984.
3. Maurice Hutt, ed., *Napoleon* (Englewood Cliffs, N.J.: Prentice-Hall, 1972), p. 151.
4. The three books, all authored by Burt Nanus and published by Jossey-Bass Division of Macmillan in San Francisco, are *Visionary Leadership* (1992), *The Vision Retreat: A Facilitator's Guide* (1995) and *The*

Vision Retreat: Participant's Workbook (1995).

5. Quoted in Charles M. Farkas and Phillippe DeBacker, *Maximum Leadership* (New York: Henry Holt, 1996), p. 141.

Strategy II: Meaning Through Communication

1. Richard Snyder, "Organizational Culture," in Warren Bennis et al., eds., *The Planning of Change,* 4th ed. (New York: Holt, 1985).
2. Howard Schwartz and Stan Davis, "Corporate Culture: The Hard-to-Change Values That Spell Success or Failure," *Business Week,* Oct. 17, 1980.
3. Ibid.
4. Alfred P. Sloan, Jr., *My Years with General Motors* (New York: Doubleday, 1946; Anchor, 1972).
5. Ibid., pp. 45–60.
6. J. Patrick Wright, *On a Clear Day You Can See General Motors* (Grosse Point, Mich.: Wright Enterprises, 1979), pp. 16–17.
7. Ibid., pp. 17, 18.
8. Ibid., p. 15.
9. Mary Parker Follett, *Dynamic Administration* (New York: Harper, 1941), pp. 143–44.
10. Noel Tichy and David Ulrich, "The Leadership Challenge—A Call for the Transformational Leader," *Sloan Management Review,* Fall 1984, pp. 59–68.
11. Brooke W. Tunstall, "Cultural Transition at AT&T," *Sloan Management Review,* Fall 1983, p. 9.
12. Ibid., p. 10.
13. Sun-tzu, *The Art of War,* edited by James Clavell (New York: Delacorte, 1980), p. 5.
14. Tichy and Ulrich, op. cit.
15. *Johnson & Johnson,* Harvard Business School Case #0-384-053, prepared in 1983 by Arvind Bhambri, our col-

league at USC's School of Business Administration. The case is distributed by the HBS Case Services, Harvard Business School, Boston MA 02163. This quote is from p. 4.

16. Ibid., p. 5.
17. Ibid.
18. Ibid., p. 6.
19. Tunstall, op. cit., p. 11.

Strategy III: Trust Through Positioning

1. John W. Gardner, *On Leadership* (New York: Free Press, 1990).

Strategy IV: The Deployment of Self

1. Donald N. Michael, "Planning—And Learning from It," in John M. Richardson, Jr., ed., *Making It Happen* (Washington, D.C.: U.S. Association for the Club of Rome, 1982), pp. 175–80.
2. James W. Botkin, Elmandjra Mahdi, and Malitza Mircea, *No Limits to Learning* (New York: Pergamon, 1979), p. 10.
3. James MacGregor Burns, *Leadership* (New York: Harper & Row, 1978), p. 380.
4. Alfred P. Sloan, Jr., *My Years with General Motors* (New York: Doubleday, 1946; Anchor, 1972).
5. W. Brooke Tunstall, "Cultural Transition at AT&T," *Sloan Management Review*, Fall 1983.
6. Audrey Choi, "Stacked DEC: Digital's New Attitude Toward Old Enemies Puts It Back in Game," *Wall Street Journal*, April 9, 1996, p. A10.
7. Burns, op cit., p. 117.
8. Jeff Cole, "Gentle Persuasion: New CEO at Hughes

Studied Its Managers, Got Them on His Side," *Wall Street Journal*, March 30, 1993, p. A6.

9. Daniel Hertzberg, "Citicorp Leads Field in Its Size and Power—And in Its Arrogance," *Wall Street Journal*, May 11, 1984, p. 1.

10. Jan J. Erteszek, "The Common Venture Enterprise: A Western Answer to the Japanese Art of Management," *New Management* 1 (1983): 5.

11. Michael, 1982, op. cit.

12. James Brian Quinn, *Strategies for Change* (Homewood, Ill.: Irwin, 1980).

13. Important new concepts of organizational learning have been developed at much greater length in a landmark book by Peter M. Senge called *The Fifth Discipline* (New York: Doubleday, 1990).

Taking Charge: Leadership and Empowerment

1. John W. Gardner, "The Antileadership Vaccine," *Annual Report of the Carnegie Corporation* (New York: Carnegie Corporation, 1965), p. 12.

2. The phrases "transformative leadership" and "transactional leadership" come from James MacGregor Burns's seminal book *Leadership* (New York: Harper & Row, 1978), chaps. 3 and 4.

3. Cited in Lovett H. Weems, Jr., *Church Leadership* (Nashville: Abingdon Press, 1993), p. 38.

4. James O'Toole, *Leading Change* (San Francisco: Jossey-Bass, 1995).

5. This anecdote was taken from an article about Mike Nichols by Barbara Gelb: "The Director's Art," *New York Times Magazine*, May 27, 1984, p. 29.

6. See Warren Bennis, *On Becoming a Leader* (Reading: Addison-Wesley, 1989), and Warren Bennis and Joan Goldsmith, *Learning to Lead* (Reading: Addison-Wesley, 1994.

INDEX